A Warrior Within, A Chronic Illness

The Warrior Mom's Guide to Thriving with Sickle Cell Anemia & Chronic Resilience

Author Shaundra M. G. Harris

A Warrior Within, A Chronic Illness

The Warrior Mom's Guide to Thriving with Sickle Cell Anemia & Chronic Resilience

Author Shaundra M. G. Harris

Shaun The Mom Publishing

© 2025 Shaundra M. G. Harris. All rights reserved.

Paperback ISBN 978-1-969446-00-9

Hardcover ISBN 978-1-969446-01-6

First Edition

No part of this publication may be reproduced, stored in a retrieval system, or transmitted in any form without written permission from the author, except by reviewers or educators using brief quotations with proper citation.

Publisher Shaun The Mom Publishing

Printed in the United States.

www.shaunthemom.com

Disclaimer

The information contained in Warrior Within is provided for inspirational, educational, and informational purposes only. The author is not a licensed medical doctor, mental health professional, attorney, or financial advisor. Nothing in this book should be considered a substitute for professional medical advice, diagnosis, treatment, counseling, legal services, or financial planning.

Always seek the advice of your physician, therapist, attorney, or other qualified professional with any questions you may have regarding your health, well-being, or personal circumstances. Never disregard professional advice or delay in seeking it because of something you have read in this book.

While every effort has been made to ensure the accuracy of the information presented, the author and publisher make no warranties, express or implied, about the completeness, reliability, or suitability of the content. The author and publisher disclaim any liability, loss, or risk incurred directly or indirectly from the use or application of any material in this book.

This book includes personal stories, reflections, and faith-based encouragement. The spiritual insights shared are based on the author's personal beliefs and experiences and are not intended to replace your personal relationship with God, your own study of Scripture, or the guidance of trusted spiritual leaders.

By reading this book, you acknowledge and agree that you are solely responsible for your choices, actions, and outcomes.

" To my children, Aoki, Layla, Jayden and Nia -who are the reason I build."

To my sister, Erica -a Sickle Cell Warrior.

May you rest peacefully.

Hello

Let me start with this: I see you.

I see the strength it takes to get up each day, care for your children, manage your home, and keep moving—even when your body pleads for rest. Motherhood alone is a monumental task. Add the weight of a chronic illness like sickle cell anemia, and it can feel like you're waging an invisible war no one else truly sees. Trust me—I know that struggle.

And I want you to know you are not alone.

There are countless warrior moms like you—women who love fiercely, nurture endlessly, and quietly fight daily battles with chronic illness. Sickle Cell may shape your journey, but it does not define your worth. It's a part of your story, but never the whole story.

Whether you're managing pain crises, fatigue, or the emotional weight that comes with chronic illness, know this:

You can still thrive.

With the right tools, mindset, and support, it is absolutely possible to live a joyful, purposeful, empowered life. This book is for you—the mother who shows up every day, even when it's hard.

Together, we'll explore how to protect your peace, nurture your body, balance your responsibilities, and fuel your spirit. You'll find practical strategies, heartfelt encouragement, and honest reflections from my own journey—from hospital visits to moments of joy and everything in between.

This isn't just about surviving.

It's about awakening the warrior within—that inner strength that may feel buried but has never left you.

As warrior moms, we do more than just get through the day. We rise. We create joy, stability, and legacy for our families. Yes, we face illness, exhaustion, depression, and financial strain—but through it all, we thrive.

There's no perfect roadmap. But within these pages, you'll find insight, support, and sisterhood. To help you take back control—of your health, your home, and your life.

From handling a pain crisis to getting dinner on the table or navigating insurance calls, you'll learn to fight with grace, lead with love, and live as the warrior you already are.

This is more than a mother's story through chronic illness.

This is a warrior's journey—a path of resilience, healing, and transformation.

Yes, even in a world where laundry pods double as ninja stars and the dishes never end—we've got this.

Welcome, sister, to your healing.

Welcome to your strength.

Welcome to the Thrive Hive.

Table of Contents

A Warrior's Journey: My Story as a Sickle Cell Warrior 2

Facing the "How" – Faith, Fire & Forward Motion 7

Part I: Understanding Sickle Cell Disease 10

  Chapter 1: What Is Sickle Cell Anemia? 11

  Chapter 2: Living With & Learning About Sickle Cell .. 18

  Chapter 3: The Diagnosis Doesn't Define You 21

  Chapter 4: Living with Intention 25

Part II: Living with Sickle Cell Disease 29

  Chapter 5: What is a Sickle Cell Crisis? 30

  Chapter 6: What Causes a Crisis? 34

  Chapter 7: Reducing Duration & Frequency of Crises . 38

  Chapter 8: Common Health Concerns Beyond Crises. 42

Part III: Managing Pain Like a Warrior 47

  Chapter 9: Types of Pain 48

  Chapter 10: Non-Medical Approaches to Pain 56

  Chapter 11: Organic Remedies 62

  Chapter 12: Medical Marijuana and SCD 68

Part IV: Everyday Wellness for Moms 74

  Chapter 13: Diet and Nutrition 75

  Chapter 14: Staying Active with Chronic Illness 81

  Chapter 15: Mind-Body Tools: Yoga, Meditation, and Breathing 90

  Chapter 16: Self-Care–Hair, Skin, and Nail Health 98

Part V-A: Managing the Homefront 112

  Chapter 17: Managing Time with Chronic Illness 113

  Chapter 18: Housekeeping with Chronic Fatigue 118

Chapter 19: Budgeting on a Medical Journey 124
Chapter 20: Managing Debt 131
Chapter 21: Grocery Shopping & Meal Prepping 136

Part V-B: Parenting and Education......................... 142
Chapter 22: Thriving at Home with Littles 143
Chapter 23: Navigating School with Strength 147
Chapter 24: Homeschooling with a Chronic Illness .. 151

Part VI: Emotional Health & Mental Well-Being . 160
Chapter 25: Emotional & Psychological Journey 161
Chapter 26: Coping and Thriving: What Helps 169
Chapter 27: Stress and Sickle Cell Anemia 173
Chapter 28: Stress Management and Well-Being....... 177
Chapter 29: Setting Boundaries 184
Reflection: Your Mental & Emotional Check-In 189

Part VII: Relationships and Family Dynamics..... 192
Chapter 30: Being Present When You're Not Well 193
Chapter 31: Loving Someone with Chronic Illness 199
Chapter 32: Romance & Chronic Illness 203
Chapter 33: Grief, Loss and Chronic Illness 210

Part VIII: Intimacy, Fertility & Sexual Health 220
Chapter 34: Family Planning with Sickle Cell 221
Chapter 35: Menstrual Health and Sickle Cell 224
Chapter 36: Pregnancy and Sickle Cell 229
Chapter 37: My Pregnancy Journeys with SCD 230
Chapter 38: Birth Control and Sickle Cell 243
Chapter 39: Health Benefits of Birth Control............. 246
Chapter 40: Understanding Male Health in SCD 251

Part IX: Mastering the Healthcare Maze 260
Chapter 41: Navigating Healthcare Systems 261
Chapter 42: Discrimination in Healthcare 269
Chapter 43: Coping with Discrimination & Stigma 273
Chapter 44: Being a Proactive Patient 278
Chapter 45: Hospital Preparedness Guide 283
Chapter 46: Future of Sickle Cell Treatments 291

Part X: Thriving Beyond the Diagnosis 300
Chapter 47: Working with Chronic Illness 301
Chapter 48: Workplace Support & Accommodations 307
Chapter 49: Maintaining Work 314
Chapter 50: College & Career with Chronic Illness.... 319
Chapter 51: Travel Tips for SCD Warriors 326

Part XI: Advocacy and Awareness 333
Chapter 52: Becoming an Advocate 334
Chapter 53: Advocacy and Education 338
Chapter 54: Spreading Awareness in Schools & Communities 339

Part XII: Financial and Legal Survival Guide 341
Chapter 55: Financial Assistance and Resources 342
Chapter 56: Legal Rights and Protections 347

Keep Pushing, Mama-You've Got This 349
A Blessing Over You, Warrior Mama 351
Book Club & Group Discussion Questions 353
Helpful Resources for Moms Living with SCD 354
With Deepest Gratitude 355
About the Author 356

A Warrior's Journey: My Story as a Sickle Cell Warrior

"Your story may begin with struggle, but it doesn't have to end there. Healing starts with truth—and the courage to speak it."

My story begins with a little girl who learned early on to push pain aside. I thought life would be easier if I just pretended everything was fine.

Both my younger sister, Erica, and I were diagnosed with sickle cell anemia. From birth, we were treated with penicillin, pain medication, hydration, and blood transfusions. After one particular hospital stay that included a transfusion, I made a vow: I would never go back. I was just a child, but I decided right then that I would not be sick.

Erica was different. She spoke up during her crises and got the care she needed. Me? I stayed quiet. I ignored my pain so I could keep doing the things I loved—playing basketball, running track, being outside with friends. Because when you're that young, being sick means missing out. It means hospitals, needles, and medications. So, I denied it. I told myself I didn't have sickle cell. I pushed it away.

That denial became a way of life. As I got older, the consequences grew. I skipped medications, avoided doctors, and honestly, I was a terrible patient. Even after several serious hospitalizations, I kept pretending I was fine.

But in 2015, reality crashed in. I lost my sister, Erica. She was only 26 when she died—suddenly and unexpectedly—from sickle cell complications. At the time, I was pregnant with my youngest child and caring for my toddler son, who also had significant health challenges.

Losing Erica was devastating. I never imagined I'd be planning my little sister's funeral. Still, instead of facing my grief, I buried myself in responsibilities and pushed my own health even further to the side. I had so many people depending on me, that I forgot to care for myself.

Then came 2021, just to remind me how important it is to prioritize self-care. I collapsed outside my workplace, nearly blacking out. My supervisor, Olivia—an angel in disguise—rushed to my side and called the paramedics. That moment changed everything. Her care and quick action may have saved my life.

In the months that followed, everything unraveled. I lost my health, my career, my income, and ended an almost fifteen-year relationship. I even met with lawyers about bankruptcy, surrendered my truck after a car accident, and struggled to feed my kids. I went from "having it all" to being sick, broke, and alone.

That day outside work, I had tried to push through. My chest hurt, I was exhausted, and I could barely breathe. I was already on probation for attendance, so missing work felt impossible. I did not want to call Olivia, my manager. To say I couldn't make it in, right before my shift was to start. I was terrified I'd lose my new job. God had other plans, before I could even clock in, I collapsed. I had to call in.

Olivia heard the distress in my voice and told me to go to the emergency room. I insisted I'd just go home and rest. Thank God she didn't listen when I said I'd be fine. As I sat on the curb trying to catch my breath, Olivia called the ER department.

The paramedics rushed me to the ER. I needed an emergency transfusion. My body was shutting down. I was diagnosed with acute chest syndrome and double pneumonia. I spent weeks in the hospital, fighting for my life—cut off from my children because of COVID-19 restrictions.

I hit rock bottom. Depression and anxiety swallowed me. I didn't want to die alone in the dark. But in the silence, I prayed. And God answered. He reminded me that I was never truly alone. Even when I didn't have the answers-I knew He did. God has the answers, but you have to be willing to ask the hard questions.

Meanwhile, even from that hospital bed, I was still Door Dashing meals and groceries to my kids. And, their father- my partner of nearly fifteen years? Oh yeah, he was busy maxing out my credit cards, dating other women, and even bought a boat—with our last bit of money, he bought a boat.

A boat. While I was fighting for my life.

What if I had died? Who would have buried me? Who would have raised our kids? My babies could have been left behind, relying on a GoFundMe for my funeral. That thought shook me to my core.

The chaos forced me to face reality: I was in this alone. The relationship I thought would carry me through the storm only added to it. In that hospital room, I made a decision: If I had to face my lowest moments by myself, then I would reach my highest moments by myself too.

When I got out, I stood on that promise. I began honoring every vow I made to God in that bed. It was time to undo the deals I'd made with denial—and with the man who kept me stuck in it.

Once home, I took inventory of everything. My body was failing. My mental and emotional health were cracked wide open. I was overwhelmed—juggling treatments and surgeries, bills, no car. I had no transportation to get my daughter to school or myself to appointments. Rideshares and rentals drained what little I had. The stress alone was triggering my symptoms.

I was in pure survival mode.

And my kids? They were watching it all. Their parents had turned—let's just be real—ghetto and toxic. That behavior may be common today, but my kids had never seen it from us in their home. Watching our breakdown, on top of my medical crisis, was traumatic. I prayed over them every single day—for strength, for healing, for peace. As a mother, I felt like a failure. I kept asking God: How did we get here? How did I let it get this bad?

But God...

He carried me. He rebuilt me. He reminded me that even in the storm, His promises still stand.

Let me tell you—when I came out of that season, I was stronger than I ever thought possible. My faith, my health, my sanity, my family—all tested. But I survived. And then? I began to thrive.

There is power in prayer. If you sit in the silence long enough, the answers will come. Have these hard conversations- with yourself, with Hod. Ask the tough questions. Write them down. Ask for clarity, for courage. And then follow through. God will help you, hunni—but you've got to face the truth and move forward. Okay, mama? Okay.

Through it all, I learned one of the most important lessons of my life:

I don't have to do this alone. And neither do you.

When I talk about resilience, it's because I've lived it. When I talk about strength, it's because I've been at rock bottom—where your body fails, your world falls apart, and you still keep going.

Sickle cell has taken so much from me. It took my sister in 2015. It nearly took me in 2021. But it also taught me how to fight. How to rebuild. How to heal.

I've lived through grief, chronic illness, emotional abuse, and financial ruin. But I'm still here. And so are you.

You don't have to walk this road alone.

You are strong enough to face the storm.

And I'm here to show you how I took back control of my health and my life—and how you can too.

...I've lived through grief, chronic illness, emotional abuse, and financial ruin. But I'm still here. And so are you.

You don't have to walk this road alone.

You are strong enough to face the storm.

And I'm here to show you how I took back control of my health and my life—and how you can too.

🦋 Pause & Reflect: A Warrior's Journey

Every warrior's journey starts with a moment of truth. Mine began in a hospital bed.

Where has your moment of truth been—and what did it teach you about your strength?

Facing the "How" – Faith, Fire & Forward Motion

Before we go any further in the book, let's do a quick exercise—and maybe start putting out some small fires (because let's be honest, there are always little fires when you're a mom). This is one of the first things I learned to do that helped in real life and in real time. So, let's get into my icebreaker—or should I say, fire extinguisher.

Let's get real—managing your health while raising kids, juggling responsibilities, and trying to thrive (not just survive) is no small feat. If you're anything like me, some days feel like you're juggling flaming swords while blindfolded. With toddlers. During a thunderstorm.

One of the most important things I've learned is to know your triggers. What sets off your sickle cell crises—or any chronic illness you're managing? What stresses you out? And more importantly: how do you manage it before it manages you?

Stress is a sneaky little villain. And for those of us with chronic illness, it's basically the arch-nemesis. Personally, I've found that my stress usually comes from one thing: the unknown. The dreaded how.

You know the one:

- How do I pay this bill?
- How do I make this work?
- How am I supposed to do ALL of this?

That innocent-looking how? is actually anxiety in disguise, and she does not come to play nice.

But here's the first tool in your toolbox: Face the "how."

Name the problem. Literally—write it down. Then, list out some possible solutions. Yes, even the wild ones. Even the "I'd need a miracle" ones. Because spoiler alert: God loves a good miracle moment.

Something magical happens when you stop letting stress swirl around in your brain and instead get it out where you can see it. Suddenly, you're not just worrying—you're working. That sense of progress will literally lighten your heart. It's like mental Febreze.

Here's the fire extinguisher strategy:

1. Write down the problem.
2. List all the solutions you can think of—no shame, no filters.
3. Choose one thing, just one, that you can try right now.
4. Do it. That's it. Start there.

You'd be amazed how often the problem starts to shift just because you took a single step.

Forward is forward.

Now, let's talk about what I call the most critical piece: mental health.

Bad stress isn't just bad—it can be deadly. Chronic illness doesn't like competition, and stress is one competitor you don't want hanging around. That's why we're going to talk about how to calm the chaos: how to pray through it, plan around it, and push past it.

Because when you finally let go of what you can't control and hand it over to God? That's when things start falling into place. Not always your plan—but always His plan. And His plan? It's better.

So, here's your invitation: Let's start by embracing the power of God. Once you learn to trust Him fully, your days will feel lighter. More peaceful. More sane. More beautiful.

You'll still have tough days—because life—but you'll also have divine strength backing you up. Everything becomes easier when you're aligned with God's plan for your life, even when things don't go according to YOUR plan. They are going according to THE plan—God's plan.

I know the battles you're facing—health battles, mom-life struggles, financial worries, relationship roller coasters. Been there. Bought the T-shirt. Probably spilled juice on it.

I've walked the road, and now I'm here to walk with you. Together, we'll find strength, hope, and ways to thrive in this beautiful, complicated life. But here's the truth: You can get through this—we're reclaiming our joy, our health, and our power.

🦬 Pause & Reflect: Faith, Fire, and Forward Motion

What "how" has been weighing on your heart lately?

Write it down, release it to God, and take one small step forward today.

Part I: Understanding Sickle Cell Disease

Chapter 1: What Is Sickle Cell Anemia?

Sickle cell anemia is a chronic, inherited blood disorder that affects how red blood cells function in the body. In a healthy person, red blood cells are soft, round, and flexible—able to move easily through the bloodstream and deliver oxygen to every part of the body.

But in someone with sickle cell anemia, these cells become stiff, sticky, and shaped like a crescent or sickle (like the curved blade used in farming).

These misshapen cells don't flow freely. Instead, they clump together and block blood vessels, leading to reduced oxygen flow, pain, and damage to vital organs over time.

Who It Affects

Sickle cell anemia is most common in people of African descent, but it also occurs in people from areas where malaria is or was common, including:

- Sub-Saharan Africa
- India
- The Middle East
- The Mediterranean (e.g., Greece, Italy, Turkey)
- Central and South America

This distribution is due to the sickle cell trait's partial protection against malaria. People who carry one copy of the gene (the trait) were more likely to survive malaria, which made the gene more common in these regions.

How It's Inherited

Sickle cell anemia is passed down in an autosomal recessive pattern. This means a child must inherit two copies of the mutated gene—one from each parent—to develop the disease.

What's the difference between the trait and the disease?

If a child inherits only one copy, they will have sickle cell trait, which usually causes no symptoms but can still be passed to the next generation.

The trait means you carry one gene (usually symptom-free); the disease means you inherited two genes and will likely have health complications.

The root cause is a mutation in the HBB gene, which affects hemoglobin—the protein in red blood cells responsible for carrying oxygen. In sickle cell anemia, this abnormal hemoglobin is called hemoglobin S (HbS). Under stress—such as dehydration, low oxygen, infection, or extreme temperatures—these cells "sickle" and break down faster, living only 10–20 days instead of the usual 120. This leads to a constant shortage of healthy red blood cells, or anemia.

Common Symptoms and Complications

No two people with sickle cell experience it exactly the same way, but common symptoms include:

- Pain Crises: Sudden episodes of sharp pain (often in the bones, chest, abdomen, or joints) due to blocked blood flow. These "crises" can last hours or days.
- Fatigue: Ongoing tiredness from chronic anemia and low oxygen levels.

- Frequent Infections: The spleen—an organ that helps fight infection—is often damaged, increasing the risk of illness.
- Swelling (Dactylitis): Painful swelling in the hands and feet, especially in infants.
- Delayed Growth and Puberty: Limited oxygen and nutrients can slow a child's development.
- Organ Damage: The heart, kidneys, liver, and lungs can suffer over time.
- Stroke: Children and adults with SCD are at risk of stroke due to blocked blood vessels in the brain.
- Vision Problems: The eyes, especially the retina, can be affected by reduced blood flow.

What Triggers a Crisis?

Several lifestyle and environmental factors can worsen symptoms:

- Dehydration
- Infection
- High stress
- Cold weather
- High altitudes
- Physical overexertion

Knowing your triggers—and how to manage or avoid them—is essential to living well with sickle cell.

Treatment Options and What's Ahead

While there's no universal cure, there are several ways to manage sickle cell and improve quality of life:

- Hydroxyurea: A daily medication that reduces pain crises and the need for transfusions.

- Blood Transfusions: Used to treat severe anemia or prevent strokes by increasing healthy red cells.

- Pain Management: Both medications and non-drug tools like hydration, warm compresses, and rest.

- Bone Marrow or Stem Cell Transplants: A potential cure, especially for children with a matched donor.

- Gene Therapy (Emerging): Recently approved options like Casgevy and Lyfgenia are offering hope for long-term cure.

What are the Types of Sickle Cell Disease

Sickle cell disease (SCD) has several subtypes based on the specific genes inherited:

- HbSS (Sickle Cell Anemia): The most severe and common type. Both parents pass on the sickle gene.

- HbSC: One sickle gene and one hemoglobin C gene. Usually milder than HbSS but still serious.

- HbSβ^+ Thalassemia: A mix of sickle cell and a mild form of thalassemia.

- HbSβ^0 Thalassemia: A more severe combination of sickle cell and thalassemia.

- Other rare variants also exist and should be discussed with your healthcare team.

Ask your doctor to share your hemoglobin electrophoresis test results so you know your specific type. Also ask about treatment options, daily pain management, transplant eligibility, and genetic risks for future children.

Why These Questions are Searched Frequently

These topics reflect the most pressing concerns for individuals living with SCD, their families, or those carrying the trait:

- Understanding inheritance mechanisms
- Evaluating risk and planning for children
- Managing daily symptoms and avoiding crises
- Exploring latest treatment breakthroughs, especially gene therapy
- Knowing long-term outlook and quality of life

Warrior Mom Reminder

Whether you're newly diagnosed or raising a child with sickle cell, remember asking questions is an act of strength. This journey can be overwhelming—but you're not alone.

Empowerment begins with knowledge.

🦋 Reflection | Affirmation | Prayer | Action
What Is Sickle Cell Anemia?

Reflection

Whether you're the one living with sickle cell or raising a child who is, questions are always part of the journey. Sometimes they're medical. Sometimes they're emotional. Sometimes you just want to know you're not alone.

Take a moment to reflect:

1. What question about sickle cell have I been afraid to ask out loud?
2. What answer brought me the most peace today?

You don't have to know everything—but you are allowed to keep learning, seeking, and growing.

Affirmation

"I may not have all the answers, but I carry strength, wisdom, and divine support through every unknown."

Say this aloud when doubt creeps in or when you feel overwhelmed by the weight of questions without answers.

Prayer

God, I lift up every warrior mom reading this right now. Thank You for the strength to live through what we don't always understand. For every question that has no clear answer, I ask for clarity. For every fear, give peace. And for every new treatment, decision, or challenge ahead, remind us that You Walk with us. Teach us to ask boldly, rest intentionally, and lean on You always. Amen.

Action Step

- Make a list of 3–5 questions you still have about sickle cell (your diagnosis, your child's care, treatment options, or long-term planning).

Bring these questions to your next doctor's appointment—or journal them and pray over them this week.

Empowered questions lead to empowered care.

Chapter 2: Living With & Learning About Sickle Cell

Living with sickle cell anemia is not an easy task—but understanding how it affects your body, emotions, and everyday life can be one of the most powerful things you ever do.

For years, I avoided my sickle cell diagnosis. I didn't take the time to understand the disease or how deeply it shaped me. It wasn't until adulthood that I realized how intertwined sickle cell was with everything—my health, my finances, my friendships, my relationships, my parenting, even my patience.

One crisis and recovery could cost me a week's salary. I'd miss birthdays, family milestones, and school events. While people thought I was just flaking, I was actually fighting for my life—sometimes facing organ failure, sometimes so depressed I could barely get out of bed.

Because I didn't understand how sickle cell impacted my temperament, my energy, and my patience, I pushed myself past my limits.

At one point, I was:

- Working 40+ hours a week on midnight shifts
- Homeschooling four children during the day
- Studying for two degrees (surgical technician and nursing)
- Managing life with a partner who was often gone, unfaithful, and financially abusive

The weight broke me down. And worse, I wasn't getting consistent medical care. That was selfish—not only to myself but to my children. I thought I was "working hard" to give them a better life. In reality, I was "working hard" at risking my life.

Looking back, I realize: sickle cell was never meant to be a curse. It was God's reminder to slow down. To live softly. To remove toxic relationships. To choose rest and peace over striving.

Now I understand—taking care of myself is not optional. It is survival. It is stewardship. It is legacy.

Whether you're newly diagnosed or have been navigating this condition for years, knowledge is one of your strongest tools.

This book is here to give you clarity and confidence—not only about what sickle cell is, but how it shapes your world as a woman, as a mother, and as a warrior.

🦋 Reflection | Affirmation | Prayer | Action
Understanding the Impact of Sickle Cell

Reflection

1. What part of living with sickle cell feels the most overwhelming right now?
2. In what ways has learning about your illness made you feel stronger or more in control?
3. How has motherhood changed the way you think about your health?

Affirmation

"I am not a burden—I am a blessing. Even on hard days, I am worthy of care, rest, and joy."

Prayer

God, thank You for giving me the strength to carry the weight of chronic illness and motherhood. When I feel exhausted, remind me that I am not alone. Teach me to care for myself with wisdom and love—so I can care for others with compassion and grace. Amen.

Action Step

Make a self-care list that honors your body: hydration, rest, nutrition, medication, boundaries. Post it where you'll see it daily. Circle one thing you will commit to this week—just for you.

Chapter 3: The Diagnosis Doesn't Define You

When you hear the words chronic illness, it can feel like the world shifts beneath your feet. Dreams blur. Fear creeps in. Questions rise like waves.

For me, it started early—I grew up with sickle cell disease. But nothing prepared me for how different it would feel as a mother. Suddenly, the stakes were higher. Could I do this? Would my body hold up? Was I enough?

It's easy to feel like your diagnosis is a prison sentence. Like it steals your identity and dictates your worth. But one of the most freeing truths I've learned is this:

My diagnosis is a part of my story—but it's not the whole story.

You are still you.

The mom who sings lullabies. The woman who dreams of laughter, peace, and purpose. You are still allowed to grieve, to hope, to feel joy.

Motherhood magnifies everything—our love, our fears, our guilt.

Add chronic illness, and the weight can feel unbearable. But here's the truth:

- You can be both brave and broken.
- You can be soft and strong.
- You can be tired and still worthy.

And,

- You don't have to be perfect to be powerful.
- You don't have to hide your hard days to be holy.
- You don't have to "overcome" everything to be enough.

This chapter is your permission slip:

1. To reclaim your worth.
2. To let go of shame.
3. To write a new chapter with compassion for the woman you are becoming.

🦋 Reflection | Affirmation | Prayer | Action
The Diagnosis Doesn't Define You

Reflection
1. Where were you when you first heard the word "sickle cell"?
2. What emotions surfaced—fear, confusion, denial, courage?
3. How has your understanding of the diagnosis shifted with time and motherhood?

Bonus Exercise
Write a letter to your younger self on diagnosis day. What would you tell her now? What strength has she shown you since that day?

Affirmation
"I am not my diagnosis. I am created with purpose, filled with resilience, and worthy of joy."

Prayer
God, thank You for seeing all of me—not just my symptoms, but my soul. Help me to remember that my value isn't based on my pain scale. You created me with intention. Even when I feel broken, I am still held, still whole, and still loved. Amen.

Action Step

Build your care team.

- List your current doctors, therapists, or supporters.
- Add one missing person.
- Make one call this week—book an appointment, ask a question, or simply say "thank you."

Chapter 4: Living with Intention

If Chapter 2 showed us the impact of sickle cell and Chapter 3 reminded us our identity is bigger than a diagnosis, then this chapter is about the how.

How do you actually live with chronic illness in a way that honors both your body and your calling?

The answer is intention.

When I ignored my health, I ended up in crisis—hospitalized, intubated, isolated. Over working my body and undervaluing my mind.

But when I slowed down, chose peace over hustle, and honored my body's limits, my whole life shifted. Living with intention has restored so much of my sanity.

As a mother who's currently thriving with a chronic illness setting my intention, on living with intention, has been game changing.

Living with intention means:
- Saying no to toxic relationships.
- Prioritizing rest without guilt.
- Creating rhythms instead of running on chaos.
- Choosing softness in a world that pressures us to be hard.

Sickle cell taught me that a "soft life" isn't laziness—it's wisdom. Stress steals oxygen. Striving steals joy. But peace, faith, and intentional living give life.

This is not about giving up. It's about giving yourself permission to thrive—on purpose.

🪶 Pause & Reflect

Living with Intention

- Where in your life are you striving instead of surrendering?
- What's one way you can create peace in your daily routine?
- How might choosing rest today actually help you show up stronger tomorrow?

Part I: Understanding Sickle Cell Disease
Reflection | Affirmation | Prayer | Action

Reflection

You've taken the first step by learning the "what," "how," and "why" of sickle cell.

Pause and ask yourself:

- What new truth about sickle cell do I now carry with me?
- How has understanding the medical, emotional, and spiritual side of this illness changed how I see myself—or my child?
- What fears do I need to surrender, and what strengths can I celebrate?

Affirmation

"I am more than my diagnosis. Knowledge is power, and wisdom is freedom. I will live with intention, compassion, and strength."

Prayer

Heavenly Father, thank You for the wisdom to understand my body and the courage to face this illness with open eyes and a faithful heart. Remind me that no diagnosis can define me more than Your love does. May this knowledge not bring fear, but clarity and peace. Guide me to walk in intention, rest, and purpose. Amen.

Action

- Write down one fact or truth from this section that brought you peace. Post it where you can see it daily.
- Share one thing you've learned with a loved one, helping them better understand your journey.
- Choose one intentional step this week—whether it's drinking more water, saying "no" to something that drains you, or carving out 10 minutes for rest.

Part II: Living with Sickle Cell Disease

Chapter 5: What is a Sickle Cell Crisis?

A sickle cell crisis is a sudden episode of intense pain caused by sickle-shaped red blood cells blocking blood flow through small vessels. When blood flow is interrupted, oxygen cannot reach tissues and organs. This lack of oxygen leads to pain, tissue damage, and sometimes serious complications.

As someone living with sickle cell, I can tell you—no two crises are ever exactly the same. Sometimes it feels like fire in my bones. Other times it sneaks up slowly, starting with aches and swelling, until the pain becomes unbearable. What looks invisible on the outside can feel like a storm raging inside.

There are several types of crises you may experience or need to watch for:

1. Painful (Vaso-occlusive) Crisis

This is the most common type of sickle cell crisis. It occurs when the sickle-shaped cells block blood flow in the vessels, causing sharp, sudden pain in the bones, chest, abdomen, or joints. The pain can last for hours or even days. Many of us require strong pain management, sometimes even hospitalization.

2. Splenic Crisis

The spleen helps filter blood and fight infection, but sickle cells can damage it. During a splenic crisis, the spleen enlarges or loses function. This can cause a dangerous drop in red blood cells (anemia) and increase infection risk. For children especially, this is one of the first serious complications parents may notice.

3. Aplastic Crisis

Triggered most often by infection, an aplastic crisis happens when the bone marrow suddenly stops making enough red blood cells. Symptoms include severe fatigue, weakness, and pale skin. It's a reminder of how fragile the balance inside our bodies can be.

4. Acute Chest Syndrome (ACS)

This is one of the most dangerous complications. ACS happens when blood flow to the lungs is blocked, or an infection sets in. Symptoms include chest pain, cough, fever, and trouble breathing. It can look like pneumonia, but it escalates quickly and requires immediate care.

5. Stroke

Sickled cells can sometimes block blood vessels in the brain, leading to stroke. This is most common in children with sickle cell, but it can happen at any age. Signs include sudden weakness, difficulty speaking, vision problems, or paralysis. A stroke is always a medical emergency.

Triggers of a Crisis

While sometimes a crisis happens without warning, there are common triggers:

- Dehydration (not enough water)
- Extreme temperatures (too hot or too cold)
- High stress or exhaustion
- Illness or infection
- High altitude or low oxygen levels

Learning to recognize your personal triggers is part of taking back control. For me, pushing my body too far—working long hours, skipping rest, or not drinking enough water—almost always leads to a crisis.

Managing and Preventing Crises

With the right care and lifestyle adjustments, many crises can be reduced or managed:

- Stay hydrated (water is medicine).
- Take prescribed medications (like hydroxyurea) consistently.
- Keep up with medical appointments and labs.
- Use blood transfusions when necessary.
- Rest and honor your limits.
- Seek urgent care if symptoms escalate.

Even with the best planning, crises may still happen. But preparation, support, and knowledge can make them less overwhelming.

Remember: a crisis doesn't define your strength—it simply reveals the fight inside you.

Reflection | Affirmation | Prayer | Action
What is a Sickle Cell Crisis?

Reflection

1. Which type of crisis have you (or your loved one) experienced most often?
2. What patterns or triggers have you noticed leading up to a crisis?
3. How do you usually cope—physically, emotionally, and spiritually—when a crisis happens?

Affirmation

"I am prepared, protected, and resilient. Even in crisis, I am not powerless."

Prayer

God, crises can feel frightening and unpredictable, but You are steady even when my body is not. Help me to prepare wisely, notice warning signs, and trust that You are with me in every storm. Surround me with support, strength, and peace in times of pain. Amen.

Action Step

Create a Crisis Care Plan:

- Write down your triggers, emergency contacts, current medications, and preferred hospital.
- Share it with family, friends, or caregivers so you don't have to explain everything in the middle of a crisis.

Chapter 6: What Causes a Crisis?

(aka "Why did my body betray me this time?")

In my personal experience? Anything and everything. Just kidding—but not really. Sickle cell doesn't play fair, and sometimes it feels like even looking at the weather wrong can trigger a crisis.

The truth is, anything that throws your body off balance—too much or too little of something—can set off a crisis. It's like your body is walking a tightrope and life keeps trying to knock it over.

Take temperature, for example. You can't be too hot, and you definitely can't be too cold. Your body needs that Goldilocks "just right" comfort level.

But guess what? You don't control the weather. And unless you have your own personal thermostat bubble (or live alone—lucky you), it's hard to stay in that sweet spot.

A house full of people arguing over the AC settings? Recipe for pain. Exposed to the "wrong" temperature for too long? Boom—welcome to Crampville.

Why does this matter? Because sickle cell crises happen when your red blood cells change shape—literally sickling—due to stress, dehydration, or low oxygen.

These sickled cells are sticky and stiff. They clog your blood vessels like rush-hour traffic, cutting off oxygen and causing intense pain.

Common Triggers That Can Start a Crisis

1. Dehydration

Drink your water! When your body is dehydrated, blood thickens, and sickle cells are more likely to clump and block blood vessels.

2. Infections

Even a minor cold can be a big deal. Illnesses like colds, flu, or other infections increase oxygen demand and inflammation, triggering a crisis.

3. Stress

Physical or emotional stress (because apparently your body can't tell the difference) can increase oxygen demand and affect immune function.

4. Extreme Temperatures

Cold constricts blood vessels; heat can cause dehydration. Both extremes increase crisis risk.

5. Low Oxygen Levels

High altitudes or poor air quality reduce oxygen in the blood. Intense physical activity can also lower oxygen levels, increasing the chance of sickling.

6. Poor Blood Flow

Anything that slows circulation (like lying still for long periods) can trigger blockages.

7. Fatigue

Overexertion and extreme exhaustion reduce oxygen delivery and trigger crises.

8. Blood Loss

Injury, surgery, or menstruation lowers red blood cell count, making oxygen delivery more difficult.

9. Pregnancy

Hormonal changes and increased oxygen demand can trigger crises, especially without consistent medical care.

10.   Alcohol & Smoking

Both cause dehydration, reduce circulation, and lower oxygen levels.

11. Lack of Sleep

Insufficient rest increases stress and fatigue, reducing oxygen delivery and triggering sickling. Sleep is essential for recovery and sustaining life.

Bottom line: living with sickle cell is like managing a full-time internal chemistry set. Unfortunately, the chemicals don't always behave.

But knowledge is power. Knowing your personal triggers can help you avoid a lot of drama (not all—but we take the wins where we can). Preventive care—staying hydrated, managing stress, avoiding extreme temperatures, monitoring health, and regular checkups—makes a difference.

🦋 Reflection | Affirmation | Prayer | Action

Understanding My Crisis Triggers

Reflection

1. Which triggers on this list have affected you most in the past?
2. Are there patterns you notice before a crisis occurs?
3. How does stress or fatigue show up in your body before a crisis?

Affirmation

"I am in tune with my body, aware of my triggers, and capable of protecting my health."

Prayer

God, thank You for the wisdom to recognize my triggers and the strength to act before a crisis begins. Guide me to care for my body with intention, rest when I need it, and stay alert to the signs You place before me. Amen.

Action Step

Create a personal "trigger checklist."

- Write down your known triggers.
- Note preventive steps for each.
- Keep this checklist somewhere visible—phone, fridge, or journal—and review it weekly.

Chapter 7: Reducing Duration & Frequency of Crises

Managing a sickle cell crisis and helping to shorten its duration or reduce pain intensity involves a combination of medical treatment, self-care strategies, and prompt intervention.

While there is no universal cure for sickle cell anemia, there are several approaches that can improve symptoms, reduce complications, and enhance quality of life.

Over time, you'll discover what works best for you—it may be a combination of strategies. Communicate with your healthcare provider, and don't hesitate to speak up with questions or concerns.

Ways to Combat or Reduce a Crisis

Seek Immediate Medical Attention

- Pain Relief: Follow your doctor's recommendations for medications, including opioids or NSAIDs, and communicate clearly about pain levels.
- Hydration: IV fluids help rehydrate and thin the blood.
- Blood Transfusions: In severe cases, transfusions increase healthy red blood cells to improve oxygen delivery.

Hydration

- Drink plenty of water and electrolyte solutions.
- Limit alcohol and caffeine, which can dehydrate you.

Heat Therapy
- Use warm compresses or a heating pad on painful areas.
- Take warm baths to soothe muscle aches.

Pain Management
- Over-the-counter medications for mild pain.
- Prescription options, including hydroxyurea, for severe or frequent crises.

Oxygen Therapy
- Supplemental oxygen may be necessary if lungs are affected, such as in acute chest syndrome.

Rest
- Limit physical activity during a crisis. Overexertion can worsen pain.

Avoid Cold
- Keep warm with blankets, warm clothing, and avoid cold drafts.

Prevent Infections
- Treat infections promptly with antibiotics or antivirals.
- Stay up-to-date with vaccinations.

Use Hydroxyurea (If prescribed)
- Regular use can reduce the frequency and severity of crises by increasing fetal hemoglobin.

Stress Management
- Practice deep breathing, relaxation exercises, or meditation.

Blood Transfusions / Exchange (Severe Cases)

- Used for acute anemia or complications like acute chest syndrome.

Follow-Up Care

- Regular checkups, monitoring triggers, adjusting medications, and prevention measures.

Monitor for Complications

- Watch for signs of stroke, organ damage, or acute chest syndrome.

Healthy Lifestyle

- Balanced diet, vitamins, low-intensity exercise, avoid smoking and alcohol.

Psychological Support

- Therapy or support groups can help manage the emotional and mental strain.

Prompt and effective management during a crisis is crucial. Long-term strategies, like hydroxyurea and regular checkups, reduce the frequency of crises and improve overall health.

🦬 Reflection | Affirmation | Prayer | Action

Shortening Crises

Reflection

- Which strategies have helped you the most during past crises?
- Which areas need improvement in your routine or preparation?
- Are there triggers you could address before the next crisis occurs?

Affirmation

"I honor my body's needs and take intentional steps to reduce pain and support my health."

Prayer

God, give me wisdom and foresight to manage crises effectively. Help me stay proactive in my self-care, trust my care team, and remember that I am not alone. Guide my steps to health, comfort, and strength. Amen.

Action Step

- Create a Crisis Care Checklist: hydration, medications, warmth, rest, support system.
- Keep supplies ready: meds, heating pad, journal, emergency contacts.
- Schedule follow-ups with your healthcare provider.

Chapter 8: Common Health Concerns Beyond Crises

People with sickle cell disease can experience a wide range of health problems beyond pain crises and anemia. Abnormal sickle-shaped red blood cells can affect multiple organs and systems.

A big frustration is when medical professionals assume every symptom is sickle cell related. You know your body best—learn your baseline and advocate for yourself if something feels unusual.

Common Health Concerns

1. Pain Crises (Vaso-occlusive Crises) – Episodes of severe pain due to blocked blood flow.

2. Infections – Higher risk due to impaired immune function. Vaccines and prophylactic antibiotics help.

3. Stroke – Risk from blocked blood flow to the brain; early screening is key.

4. Acute Chest Syndrome – Lungs affected by infection or blockages; may cause severe illness.

5. Organ Damage – Kidneys, liver, heart, eyes can be affected over time.

6. Splenic Sequestration – Sudden drop in hemoglobin from spleen involvement; can be life-threatening.

7. Leg Ulcers – Poor circulation may lead to chronic, slow-healing ulcers.

8. Bone and Joint Problems – Blocked blood flow can lead to bone death or arthritis.

9. Gallstones – Excess bilirubin can form stones in the gallbladder.//
10. Pulmonary Hypertension – High blood pressure in lungs due to chronic low oxygen.
11. Delayed Growth / Puberty – Common in children with sickle cell disease.
12. Anemia – Persistent fatigue and weakness due to low red blood cell count.
13. Mental Health Issues – Anxiety, depression, and stress are common; support is essential.
14. Infertility – Reproductive complications may occur in men and women.
15. Pregnancy Complications – Higher risks for both mother and baby; requires specialized care.

Regular check-ups, preventive care, and early intervention are key to managing complications and improving quality of life.

🦬 Reflection | Affirmation | Prayer | Action
Beyond Crises

Reflection
- Which of these complications are most concerning to you?
- How well do you monitor your body for changes outside of crises?
- What steps could you take to prevent or address these issues early?

Affirmation
"I am attentive to my body and proactive in caring for all aspects of my health."

Prayer
God, give me awareness of my body and the wisdom to act early when concerns arise. Surround me with knowledge, care, and the right support to thrive beyond my crises. Amen.

Action Step
- Schedule preventive screenings and regular checkups.
- Track symptoms or unusual changes in a health journal.
- Identify support resources—medical, emotional, and spiritual—that help you manage overall health.

Part II: Living with Sickle Cell Disease
🦋 Reflection | Affirmation | Prayer | Action

Reflection

You've just explored the heart of daily life with sickle cell—the crises, the triggers, the strategies, and the concerns that stretch beyond pain.

Pause for a moment and ask yourself:

- What new strategies or truths stood out to me in this section?
- How does recognizing my triggers help me feel more in control?
- What fears still feel heavy, and what steps of preparation could lighten the load?

Affirmation

"I honor my body's wisdom. I am not powerless—I am prepared, supported, and equipped to live with strength and resilience."

Prayer

God, thank You for walking with me through the stormy moments of sickle cell and the quiet in-between. Thank You for giving me wisdom to see my triggers, courage to manage my health, and hope beyond the pain. Teach me to prepare wisely, rest deeply, and advocate boldly. May my life reflect strength, even in weakness, and peace, even in crisis. Amen.

Action

- Review your Crisis Care Plan and update it if needed.
- Create a Preventive Care Calendar (hydration, rest, meds, checkups) and commit to one intentional step this week.
- Share one coping strategy or preventive tip from this section with a family member, friend, or caregiver to help them support you better.

Part III: Managing Pain Like a Warrior

Chapter 9: Types of Pain

Listen, baby, with pain, there's no gain -no one's got time for that. Mama, if you're hurting and can't figure it out on your own, take yourself to the hospital. If it's dragging on with no relief, hospital. If you've tried everything and nothing's working, hospital. If you don't understand what's going on, hospital.

You didn't go to medical school, but they did! Let those folks help you get through this faster so you can get back to your life. Don't sit around at home, miserable for days, even weeks-it's just silly when you can get the professional care you need to move past this.

Go get the help you deserve!

Pain can be categorized in various ways, especially when considering conditions like sickle cell disease. Understanding the different types of pain can help in managing and addressing it more effectively.

Below are some categories of pain that individuals with sickle cell disease might experience:

1. **Acute Pain**

Description: Acute pain is sudden, sharp, and typically short-lived. In sickle cell disease, acute pain often occurs during a pain crisis, when sickled red blood cells block blood flow and cause tissue ischemia (lack of oxygen to tissues).

Causes:

- Vaso-occlusive crises (blocked blood flow).
- Infections or fever.

- Trauma or injury.
- Surgery or medical procedures.

Management: This type of pain often requires immediate medical attention, such as pain medication, hydration, and sometimes hospitalization.

2. Chronic Pain

Description: Chronic pain persists over a long period (usually over 3 to 6 months). It can be a result of ongoing sickle cell damage to organs (like the bones, joints, and spleen) or damage caused by repeated crises.

Causes:

- Long-term damage to bones and joints (e.g., avascular necrosis).
- Ongoing tissue damage from repeated vaso-occlusive episodes.
- Chronic inflammation in tissues.

Management: Chronic pain may require ongoing pain management, including medication (e.g., low-dose opioids, NSAIDs), physical therapy, lifestyle modifications, and psychological support.

3. Nociceptive Pain

Description: This type of pain occurs when tissue is injured, leading to activation of pain receptors. It can be either somatic (musculoskeletal) or visceral (internal organs).

Causes:

- Muscle or joint pain during a sickle cell crisis.
- Inflammation in the chest or abdomen.

Management: Pain relief is often managed with NSAIDs, physical therapy, and, in some cases, opioids.

4. Neuropathic Pain

Description: Neuropathic pain arises when there is nerve damage or dysfunction, resulting in a burning, tingling, or stabbing sensation. In sickle cell disease, nerves can be affected by decreased blood flow during crises or from other complications.

Causes:

- Nerve compression or damage from sickle cell-related complications like stroke or spinal cord infarction.
- Damage to peripheral nerves or the nervous system due to lack of oxygen in tissues.

Management: This type of pain may require medications like gabapentin, pregabalin, or antidepressants (like amitriptyline) and physical therapy to manage symptoms.

5. Visceral Pain

Description: Visceral pain is deep, cramping, or aching pain originating from internal organs (such as the abdomen, chest, or pelvis). It can sometimes be difficult to pinpoint.
Causes:

- Pain from spleen enlargement or infarction (due to sickle cell).
- Pain related to the liver, kidneys, or lungs from blood flow obstruction.
- Abdominal pain from sickle cell crises affecting organs like the intestines.

Management: This pain often requires medications like opioids, antispasmodics, or NSAIDs for relief.

6. Bone Pain

Description: Bone pain, often described as deep or dull, is common in sickle cell disease. It is typically caused by blocked blood flow in the bone marrow, leading to tissue damage.

Causes:

- Avascular necrosis (loss of blood supply to bone tissue).
- Painful crises affecting the bones (especially in areas like the back, hips, and joints).

Management: Bone pain may require stronger pain relief, including opioids or long-term treatments like bisphosphonates, and occasionally surgery if avascular necrosis is present.

7. Musculoskeletal Pain

Description: This type of pain involves the muscles, joints, and connective tissues. It can be localized or widespread, depending on the condition.

Causes:

- Muscle cramps and stiffness during or after a pain crisis.
- Joint pain from inflammation and damage.
- Repetitive strain or overuse of joints and muscles.

Management: Muscle pain can be managed with stretching, physical therapy, massage, NSAIDs, and sometimes opioids if severe.

8. Referred Pain

Description: Referred pain occurs when pain is felt in a part of the body that is not the actual source of the pain. For instance, pain in the chest during a sickle cell crisis may actually originate in the abdomen or spleen.

Causes:

- Problems with internal organs, such as the spleen or liver, that cause pain in other areas.
- Blockages in blood flow leading to pain being referred to the chest or back.

Management: Identifying the source of the pain is crucial to treating referred pain. Pain relief will typically target the underlying cause.

9. Psychogenic Pain

Description: This type of pain is linked to emotional, psychological, or behavioral factors. Stress, anxiety, and depression can exacerbate the experience of pain or make it harder to manage.

Causes:

- Emotional or psychological distress from dealing with chronic illness.
- Anxiety or depression related to living with sickle cell disease.

Management: Managing psychogenic pain often requires a holistic approach, including cognitive-behavioral therapy (CBT), counseling, stress management techniques, and support groups.

10. Breakthrough Pain

Description: Breakthrough pain refers to sudden, intense pain that occurs despite the person being on a regular pain management regimen. It can come on unexpectedly and can be quite severe.

Causes:

- Pain crises breaking through regular pain management.
- Sudden worsening of pain despite ongoing treatment.

Management: Short-acting pain medications, additional hydration, or interventions like heat or cold therapy may be necessary to manage breakthrough pain.

11. Post-Surgical Pain

Description: Pain that arises after surgery, which could be related to sickle cell disease treatment or other surgeries (such as a joint replacement for avascular necrosis).

Causes:

- Healing after bone or organ surgeries.
- Inflammation or tissue injury related to surgery.

Management: Post-surgical pain is typically managed through a combination of medications (opioids, NSAIDs), physical therapy, and rest.

12. Phantom Pain

Description: Phantom pain occurs in an area where tissue has been lost or amputated, but the individual still feels pain in that area. Although it's not as common in sickle cell disease, it may occur after surgery or severe complications that result in limb amputation.

Causes:

- Nerve damage that sends pain signals to the brain even after the limb or tissue is no longer there.

Management: Phantom pain can be managed with therapies like mirror therapy, certain medications (e.g., anticonvulsants or antidepressants), and nerve blocks.

Understanding these different types of pain can help in identifying the cause and finding appropriate treatments. In SCD, pain often comes from multiple sources. It's important to address each aspect "whether it's acute or chronic, visceral or musculoskeletal" in a comprehensive pain management plan.

Tracking Your Pain: The Power of a Pain Diary

Keeping a pain diary can help you and your doctors better understand triggers, patterns, and treatment effectiveness.

Pain Diary Template:
- Date & Time
- Pain Location
- Pain Level (0–10)
- Description (sharp, throbbing, burning, etc.)
- Trigger (weather, stress, period, etc.)
- What Helped? (medication, rest, hydration, etc.)

"What gets measured gets managed." A pain journal gives your experience a voice in the doctor's office.

🕊 Reflection | Affirmation | Prayer | Action
Types of Pain

Reflection

- Which type of pain do you experience most often—acute, chronic, nerve, or bone?
- How do you usually describe your pain to others (or your doctor)?
- Does your pain have a pattern—time of day, weather, stress, or other triggers?

Affirmation

"My pain has patterns, but it does not have power over me. I recognize it, track it, and trust myself to seek the help I need."

Prayer

Lord, you know every detail of my pain—where it shows up and how it feels. Give me courage to face it and wisdom to name it. Help me use the tools You've provided—medical care, journaling, and support—without fear or shame. Amen.

Action Step

- Begin a pain diary this week. Track pain location, level (0–10), triggers, and what helps.
- Circle the pain type that most affects you today. Write one way you can respond differently next time it appears.

Chapter 10: Non-Medical Approaches to Pain

Managing pain associated with sickle cell disease (SCD) non-medically can be incredibly important for improving quality of life, especially during crises or times when medication might not fully manage the pain.

Non-medical approaches can help in conjunction with medical treatments and can sometimes provide immediate relief or long-term benefits.

Here are several strategies that can help:

1. Heat Therapy

- Warm Compresses: Applying heat to painful areas can help relax muscles, increase blood flow, and reduce pain during a sickle cell crisis. A warm towel, heating pad, or warm water bottle can be used on joints or muscles where pain is concentrated.
- Warm Baths: Soaking in a warm bath can help relax the body, ease muscle tension, and provide comfort. Sometimes adding Epsom salts or essential oils like lavender can enhance relaxation.

2. Hydration

- Stay Hydrated: Dehydration is a known trigger for pain crises in sickle cell patients, so keeping the body well-hydrated is essential. Drinking plenty of water helps prevent the sickle-shaped cells from clumping together, which can reduce the likelihood of a painful crisis.

- Electrolyte Solutions: Sometimes, sports drinks or homemade electrolyte solutions can be helpful for maintaining hydration, particularly if dehydration is due to sweating or exertion.

3. **Relaxation and Stress Management Techniques**
    - Deep Breathing Exercises: Deep breathing can reduce stress, which is a common trigger for pain in individuals with sickle cell. Techniques like diaphragmatic breathing (breathing from the belly) or guided deep breathing exercises can help calm the body.
    - Meditation and Mindfulness: Practicing mindfulness or guided meditation techniques can help individuals focus on the present moment, reduce stress, and distract from pain.
    - Progressive Muscle Relaxation (PMR): This technique involves tensing and then relaxing different muscle groups in the body, helping to reduce muscle tension that may accompany pain.

4. **Distraction Techniques**
    - Engage in Activities You Enjoy: Distraction can sometimes be an effective tool for pain management. Activities like reading, watching movies, playing video games, or listening to music can redirect the mind away from pain.
    - Creative Hobbies: Drawing, painting, knitting, or crafting can provide focus and creativity that help divert attention from discomfort.

5. **Physical Movement**
    - Gentle Stretching: Engaging in light stretching exercises can promote flexibility and reduce muscle

tightness that might exacerbate pain. It's important to stay gentle and avoid overexerting yourself.

- Yoga: Many people find relief from pain through gentle yoga poses. Certain poses can help alleviate muscle cramps and tension and promote relaxation.

- Low-Impact Exercise: Light exercises such as walking or swimming can help maintain overall health and prevent stiffness, which can reduce pain over time.

6. Acupuncture and Acupressure

- Acupuncture: Some individuals find that acupuncture helps to reduce pain and improve blood flow. It's thought that acupuncture may stimulate certain points on the body that help relieve pain and promote overall well-being.

- Acupressure: This involves applying pressure to specific points on the body to alleviate pain. Certain techniques can help relieve muscle tension and improve circulation, both of which are important for pain management in sickle cell.

7. Aromatherapy

- Essential Oils: Aromatherapy can provide emotional and physical relief. For example, lavender, peppermint, or eucalyptus oils are known for their pain-relieving and calming properties. These can be used through diffusers, in baths, or applied (diluted) to the skin.

- Massage with Oils: Using essential oils in massage therapy can help relieve muscle pain, tension, and stress. Always use a carrier oil (like coconut or olive oil) to dilute essential oils and avoid skin irritation.

8. Massage Therapy

- Gentle Massage: A gentle, soothing massage can help reduce muscle tightness, improve circulation, and offer temporary pain relief. While it's important to be cautious about applying pressure during a pain crisis, light touch may be beneficial.

- Self-Massage: Learning techniques to massage areas like the neck, back, or joints can offer relief. Tools like foam rollers or massage balls can be used for self-massage as well.

9. Cold Therapy (for Some Types of Pain)

- Cold Compresses or Ice Packs: Although heat is often used, some types of pain, like muscle inflammation or joint discomfort, might respond better to cold. Applying an ice pack wrapped in a cloth to the affected area can reduce swelling and numb the pain. However, this is usually more beneficial for pain that isn't associated with a sickle cell crisis (which can worsen with cold).

- Cryotherapy (Whole-body Cold Therapy): For some individuals, controlled exposure to cold, such as cold showers or cryotherapy chambers, may help reduce inflammation and manage pain. However, it's not suitable for everyone and should be approached with caution.

10. Mind-Body Connection and Emotional Support

- Therapeutic Journaling: Writing about your pain, thoughts, and feelings can help process emotions related to living with sickle cell and may offer mental relief. This practice can also track triggers or patterns in your pain, helping to manage and prevent future crises.

- Support Groups or Peer Support: Connecting with others who understand your experiences can provide emotional support and practical pain management strategies. Online or in-person groups can be a great resource for shared coping mechanisms.

11. Diet and Nutrition

- Anti-Inflammatory Diet: A diet rich in anti-inflammatory foods like turmeric, ginger, green leafy vegetables, berries, and fatty fish (rich in omega-3s) can help reduce the overall inflammation in the body, potentially alleviating some pain.
- Magnesium-Rich Foods: Magnesium has been shown to have muscle-relaxing properties. Consuming foods like spinach, almonds, and avocados may support muscle relaxation and reduce muscle cramps or spasms.

12. Cognitive Behavioral Therapy (CBT) and Pain Management

- CBT for Pain Management: CBT is a therapeutic approach that helps individuals reframe negative thoughts related to pain and develop coping strategies. CBT has been shown to help manage chronic pain by changing the way the brain interprets and reacts to discomfort.

These non-medical strategies can work synergistically with medical treatments to provide comprehensive pain management. It's essential to discuss these approaches with a healthcare provider to tailor them to individual needs and make sure they don't interfere with other treatments.

Reflection | Affirmation | Prayer | Action
Non-Medical Approaches to Pain

Reflection

- Which of the non-medical tools—heat, hydration, journaling, stretching, or mindfulness—resonates with you most?
- Do you feel guilty when you try rest-based tools like baths, naps, or meditation? Why or why not?
- What does your body need more of right now—rest, movement, or calm?

Affirmation

"I welcome peace into my body. I honor rest, movement, and creativity as healing tools God has placed in my hands."

Prayer

Father, thank You for simple gifts like water, breath, and movement. Show me how to use these tools to bring relief. Release guilt from my heart when I choose rest. Remind me that caring for myself is a holy act. Amen.

Action Step

- Choose one new non-medical strategy to try this week (example: heat therapy, journaling, or gentle yoga).
- Add it to your daily routine and reflect after 7 days: Did it help?

Chapter 11: Organic Remedies

For individuals with sickle cell disease (SCD) or chronic pain, there are various organic and natural options that may help manage pain.

These alternatives can complement conventional treatments but should always be discussed with a healthcare provider to ensure safety and effectiveness.

Some options include:

1. Turmeric (Curcumin)

- Properties: Turmeric contains curcumin, a compound known for its potent anti-inflammatory and pain-relieving properties.
- How it helps: It may reduce pain associated with inflammation, and there's evidence suggesting it can help with conditions like arthritis and other chronic pain disorders.
- How to use: You can incorporate turmeric into meals or take it as a supplement (usually in combination with black pepper to improve absorption).

2. Ginger

- Properties: Ginger is another powerful anti-inflammatory and antioxidant herb.
- How it helps: It may help reduce pain and inflammation, particularly in conditions like arthritis, muscle pain, and digestive pain.
- How to use: Fresh ginger can be used in teas, smoothies, or as a spice in cooking. Ginger supplements are also available.

3. Capsaicin

- Properties: Capsaicin, derived from chili peppers, has been shown to block pain signals.

- How it helps: When applied topically, it can reduce pain by depleting substance P, a neurotransmitter involved in sending pain signals.

- How to use: Capsaicin creams or ointments can be applied directly to painful areas, but it's important to follow instructions as it can cause a burning sensation.

4. CBD Oil (Cannabidiol)

- Properties: CBD, derived from the hemp plant, is non-psychoactive and has anti-inflammatory, analgesic, and muscle-relaxing properties.

- How it helps: It can help reduce chronic pain and inflammation, particularly when used in conjunction with other treatments.

- How to use: CBD can be taken in oil form, capsules, or topical creams. Be sure to choose a reputable brand and dosage.

5. Acupuncture

- Properties: Acupuncture involves inserting thin needles into specific points on the body to stimulate nerves, muscles, and connective tissue.

- How it helps: It may trigger the release of endorphins and other neurochemicals that help reduce pain and improve circulation.

- How to use: A trained acupuncturist can develop a personalized treatment plan. Some individuals experience relief after just a few sessions.

6. Epsom Salt Baths

- Properties: Epsom salt contains magnesium, which can be absorbed through the skin.
- How it helps: Magnesium may help relax muscles and ease pain and inflammation.
- How to use: Adding Epsom salts to a warm bath can help relieve muscle pain, spasms, and joint pain.

7. Essential Oils

- Properties: Certain essential oils, like peppermint, lavender, and eucalyptus, are known for their pain-relieving and anti-inflammatory properties.
- How it helps: These oils can be used for topical massage or inhaled for their calming effects on pain.
- How to use: They can be diluted in a carrier oil (like coconut or jojoba oil) and massaged into the skin or used in aromatherapy diffusers.

8. Willow Bark

- Properties: Willow bark contains salicin, a compound similar to aspirin.
- How it helps: It has anti-inflammatory and analgesic effects and has been traditionally used for pain relief.
- How to use: It can be consumed as a tea or taken in supplement form. Always consult with a healthcare provider about proper dosages.

9. Massage Therapy

- Properties: Massage promotes circulation, relaxes muscles, and releases endorphins, the body's natural painkillers.

- How it helps: It can reduce muscle tension, ease stress, and alleviate certain types of chronic pain.
- How to use: Professional massage therapy or self-massage techniques can be beneficial. You can also use a foam roller to relieve tension in specific areas.

10. Mind-Body Techniques (e.g., Meditation, Deep Breathing, Yoga)

- Properties: These techniques focus on reducing stress and promoting relaxation.
- How it helps: Chronic pain is often worsened by stress, and these practices can help manage the psychological aspects of pain. They also enhance the body's natural pain-relieving responses.
- How to use: Practices like mindfulness meditation, yoga, and deep breathing exercises can help manage pain over time.

11. Arnica

- Properties: Arnica is a plant-based remedy commonly used for bruising and pain relief.
- How it helps: It has anti-inflammatory and pain-relieving properties, especially for muscle aches, sprains, and joint pain.
- How to use: Arnica can be applied topically as a cream, gel, or ointment. It can also be taken in homeopathic pill form, but this should be done under guidance.

12. Heat and Cold Therapy

- Properties: Heat and cold therapy are simple but effective methods for managing pain.

- How it helps: Heat can relax muscles and increase blood flow, while cold can reduce inflammation and numb pain.
- How to use: A warm compress or heating pad can be applied to stiff muscles or joints, while cold packs are good for acute pain or inflammation.

Key Considerations:

- Diet: A healthy diet rich in anti-inflammatory foods like fruits, vegetables, omega-3 fatty acids (e.g., salmon, flax seeds), and whole grains can also help reduce pain levels.
- Hydration: Staying well-hydrated is important for managing sickle cell disease, as dehydration can increase the risk of pain crises.
- Consultation: Always speak with a healthcare provider, especially when dealing with conditions like sickle cell disease, to ensure the chosen methods are safe and effective for your situation.

Natural remedies can be supportive, but they should be part of a comprehensive treatment plan designed by a medical professional.

🦋 Reflection | Affirmation | Prayer | Action

Organic Remedies

Reflection

- Have you tried any natural remedies before (ginger tea, turmeric, Epsom salt baths, essential oils)? Which ones worked—or didn't?
- What concerns do you have about using organic remedies with your medical treatments?
- Which natural option feels most realistic to try right now?

Affirmation

"God created the earth with healing in mind. I can explore natural remedies with wisdom and discernment, knowing my health matters to Him."

Prayer

Lord, thank You for the natural remedies You've placed in creation. Give me discernment in choosing what is safe and right for my body. Protect me from harm and help me find balance between natural and medical care. Amen.

Action Step

- Research or ask your doctor about one natural option you'd like to explore (CBD, turmeric, Epsom salt baths, etc.).
- Write it down in your pain journal and set a safe plan for trying it.

Chapter 12: Medical Marijuana and SCD

Marijuana has been explored for its potential to help manage various types of pain, including chronic pain. Some individuals with sickle cell disease (SCD) have reported pain relief from using cannabis.

While research specific to SCD is still limited, growing evidence suggests marijuana may offer several benefits for those living with chronic pain, inflammation, and other related symptoms.

How Marijuana May Help with SCD Symptoms:

1. Pain Management

One of the most challenging aspects of SCD is the severe pain caused by "sickle cell crises." Cannabis contains active compounds like THC (tetrahydrocannabinol) and CBD (cannabidiol), both of which may help relieve pain.

- THC works by binding to cannabinoid receptors in the brain and nervous system, potentially reducing pain perception.

- CBD is believed to have anti-inflammatory and muscle-relaxing properties, which can reduce pain and tension.

When used together, THC and CBD may provide synergistic effects, offering broader pain relief, as seen in other conditions like arthritis, fibromyalgia, and neuropathy.

2. Chronic Pain Relief

Marijuana has been used to manage chronic pain in various conditions. Some studies suggest cannabis can help alter how pain is processed by the brain and reduce inflammation, making it potentially helpful for managing ongoing pain in SCD.

3. Reducing Inflammation

Chronic inflammation is a common problem in sickle cell anemia, affecting tissues and organs. CBD, in particular, has shown promise in reducing inflammation, which may help ease discomfort during and between pain episodes.

4. Improving Sleep

Pain often interferes with sleep for people with SCD. Some individuals find cannabis helpful for improving sleep quality. THC may help promote sleep and reduce insomnia, although its effects vary from person to person.

5. Relieving Muscle Spasms and Tension

Muscle spasms and tightness are common in chronic pain conditions. Cannabis may help relax muscles and relieve spasms, offering comfort during painful flare-ups.

6. Easing Nausea and Boosting Appetite

People with chronic illnesses may struggle with nausea or a lack of appetite, particularly when taking pain medications. THC has been shown to reduce nausea and stimulate appetite, which can support better nutrition and recovery.

7. Supporting Mental Health

Living with chronic pain and illness can lead to anxiety, depression, and emotional exhaustion.

- CBD may help reduce anxiety and promote emotional balance.
- THC can also elevate mood, but it should be used cautiously, as it may worsen anxiety or paranoia in some people.

Important Considerations

Side Effects and Risks

While marijuana may offer relief, it can also cause side effects such as dizziness, cognitive impairment, increased heart rate, and in some cases, worsened anxiety or mood disorders. Every person reacts differently, and what works for one may not work for another.

Legal and Medical Guidance

The legality of marijuana varies by state and country. In some places, medical marijuana is available with a prescription for conditions like SCD. It's essential to check local laws and consult with a healthcare provider before beginning use. Cannabis can interact with other medications, so professional guidance is critical.

Medical marijuana may offer promising relief for some individuals with sickle cell disease, particularly in managing pain, inflammation, sleep, and mental health. However, it's not a one-size-fits-all solution. Each person's response to cannabis is unique, and its use should always be monitored by a knowledgeable healthcare provider.

For moms navigating life with chronic illness, understanding your options—and seeking support—is a powerful step toward better quality of life.

🦬 Reflection | Affirmation | Prayer | Action
Medical Marijuana and SCD

Reflection

- How do you feel when you hear "medical marijuana"—curious, cautious, skeptical, or hopeful?
- Have you talked to your provider about whether it might be safe or legal for you?
- What are your biggest hopes (pain relief, better sleep, less anxiety) and fears (side effects, stigma) about exploring this option?

Affirmation

"I make informed choices about my health with courage and wisdom. I am not defined by stigma, but by strength and discernment."

Prayer

God, give me wisdom as I explore every option for relief. Remove fear, shame, or judgment, and replace them with peace and clarity. Surround me with trustworthy doctors, supportive loved ones, and Your presence in every decision. Amen.

Action Step

- If curious, research medical marijuana laws in your state.
- Write 3 questions to ask your provider about its risks and benefits.

Part III: Managing Pain Like a Warrior
🐃 Reflection | Affirmation | Prayer | Action

Reflection: Pain Has a Pattern

1. Where in your body does pain show up the most?
2. What time of day or season is hardest for you?
3. How do you feel when you're in pain—emotionally, mentally?

Pain is personal. Name it so you can tame it.

Affirmation: Managing Pain Like a Warrior

"I am not defined by my pain. I listen to my body, honor its needs, and treat myself with compassion. Even in discomfort, I carry strength, faith, and resilience. I choose to fight with wisdom and rest without guilt."

Prayer for Pain Relief & Endurance

Dear God,

You see every ache, every tear, and every breath I take in pain. Wrap me in Your healing presence.

Calm the fire in my body and the storm in my mind. Give me wisdom to care for myself, courage to advocate for my needs, and peace that passes understanding.

Teach me to be gentle with my limits and bold in my faith. May Your strength be made perfect in my weakness.

In Jesus' name, Amen.

Action Step: Your Pain Management Toolkit

- Start a pain journal: track location, intensity, triggers, what helps.
- List 3 non-medical tools that bring you relief (warm bath, prayer, stretching).
- Talk to your provider about new options, if your current plan isn't working.

Affirmations for a Pain Flare or Crisis

Here's a few additional affirmations your readers can repeat during a pain flare or crisis.

1. "This pain is real, but it is not forever. I breathe through it. I am held and I am healing."

2. "I am doing the best I can—and that is enough."

3. "I can rest without guilt. Rest is resistance. Rest is recovery."

4. "God is near, even now. I am never alone."

5. "My body is not my enemy. I speak to it with love."

6. "I release what I cannot control. I lean into peace one moment at a time."

7. "Each flare teaches me more about what I need. I honor my needs without shame."

Part IV: Everyday Wellness for Moms

Chapter 13: Diet and Nutrition

Eating the right foods supports overall health, boosts the immune system, improves red blood cell production, and reduces complications for those with sickle cell anemia and other chronic conditions.

You'll find nutrient categories with examples, meal ideas, and soul-food–inspired healthy alternatives. Supplements may be helpful, but always under medical supervision.

Balanced, tailored nutrition is one of the best tools for daily resilience.

1. Iron-Rich Foods

- Why? Iron is crucial for the production of red blood cells, and while sickle cell anemia causes rapid turnover of red blood cells, maintaining adequate iron levels is important. However, be careful not to over consume iron, as too much can be harmful.

Examples: Lean meats (chicken, turkey, beef), seafood (salmon, tuna), beans, lentils, fortified cereals, tofu, and leafy greens (spinach, kale).

2. Folate-Rich Foods

- Why? Folate (vitamin B9) helps the body make new red blood cells. It's especially important for individuals with sickle cell anemia, as they often have a higher turnover of red blood cells.

Examples: Dark leafy greens (spinach, collard greens, broccoli), legumes (lentils, chickpeas, beans), avocados, oranges, and fortified cereals.

3. Vitamin B12-Rich Foods

- Why? Vitamin B12 helps in the production and maturation of red blood cells, and it's essential for nerve function.

Examples: Meat, poultry, fish, eggs, dairy products, and fortified plant-based milks or cereals.

4. Vitamin C-Rich Foods

- Why? Vitamin C enhances the absorption of non-heme iron (plant-based iron) and also supports the immune system, which is vital for managing infections.

Examples: Citrus fruits (oranges, lemons), strawberries, bell peppers, tomatoes, kiwi, and broccoli.

5. Omega-3 Fatty Acids

- Why? Omega-3 fatty acids have anti-inflammatory properties, which may help reduce the frequency and severity of sickle cell pain crises. They can also support heart and brain health.

Examples: Fatty fish (salmon, mackerel, sardines), chia seeds, flaxseeds, walnuts, and hemp seeds.

6. Magnesium-Rich Foods

- Why? Magnesium helps with muscle relaxation and reduces the risk of cramps, which can be a problem for people with sickle cell anemia.

Examples: Leafy greens, nuts, seeds, whole grains, legumes, and avocados.

7. Hydrating Foods

- Why? Staying well-hydrated helps keep red blood cells from becoming too sticky and dehydrated, which can help reduce the risk of a sickle cell crisis.

Examples: Water, coconut water, herbal teas, cucumbers, watermelon, and oranges

8. Zinc-Rich Foods

- Why? Zinc supports immune function and wound healing, both of which are important for people with sickle cell anemia, as they are more vulnerable to infections.

Examples: Meat, shellfish, legumes (beans, lentils), seeds, nuts, and whole grains.

9. Foods Rich in Vitamin E

- Why? Vitamin E acts as an antioxidant, helping to reduce oxidative stress on cells, including red blood cells, which may be beneficial for people with sickle cell anemia.

Examples: Almonds, sunflower seeds, spinach, and avocado.

10. Low-Sodium Foods

- Why? Consuming too much sodium can contribute to high blood pressure and stress on the kidneys. Reducing salt intake can help protect kidney function and overall health.

Examples: Fresh, unprocessed foods such as vegetables, fruits, lean meats, and whole grains.

Foods to Limit or Avoid:

- Excessive Iron: Since individuals with sickle cell anemia may need to manage iron levels carefully, it's important not to overdo iron supplementation unless directed by a doctor. Consult your doctor if you are taking iron supplements.

- Processed Foods: Avoid overly processed foods high in unhealthy fats, sugars, and sodium, as they can contribute to inflammation and other health problems.

- Caffeine & Alcohol: These can dehydrate the body, so it's best to limit them.

Sample Meal Ideas:

1. Breakfast: A smoothie made with spinach, avocado, chia seeds, and orange juice (for vitamin C and iron absorption).

2. Lunch: Grilled chicken with quinoa, steamed broccoli, and a side of citrus fruit.

3. Dinner: Baked salmon with sweet potatoes and a kale salad with olive oil and lemon dressing.

4. Snacks: Handful of almonds, carrot sticks, or apple slices with peanut butter.

5. Southern Soul Food–Inspired Meal Idea

Dinner: Oven-baked or air-fried catfish seasoned with paprika, garlic, onion powder, and a cornmeal crust (baked instead of deep-fried to reduce unhealthy fats).

Or baked chicken seasoned to taste.

- Sides: Collard greens cooked with smoked turkey instead of pork, using garlic, onions, a splash of apple cider vinegar, and olive oil.

- Mashed sweet potatoes with cinnamon and a touch of honey or maple syrup (rich in antioxidants and vitamin A).

- Cornbread (optional): Made with whole-grain cornmeal, low-fat buttermilk, and a small amount of honey or unsweetened applesauce as a sweetener.

- Drink: Unsweetened iced hibiscus tea with lemon (rich in antioxidants and vitamin C, which helps with iron absorption).

Supplements:

Some people with SCD may benefit from specific supplements like folic acid, vitamin D, or omega-3s, but this should always be done under the guidance of a healthcare provider.

Remember, the best approach to managing sickle cell anemia with diet is one that's balanced and tailored to an individual's specific symptoms and health needs.

Working with a healthcare provider or nutritionist can help ensure that nutritional needs are met and tailored to your specific health status.

🪶 Reflection | Affirmation | Prayer | Action
Diet and Nutrition

Reflection

1. Which of the foods listed do I already enjoy and can add more often to my meals?
2. What's one small nutrition swap I could make this week (e.g., baked instead of fried, water instead of soda)?

Affirmation

"Each bite I choose with love and wisdom is fuel for my healing and strength."

Prayer

Lord, thank You for the foods You've placed in creation to nourish me. Guide my choices, strengthen my discipline, and let my meals become moments of healing. Amen.

Action

Plan one meal this week with at least one new nutrient-rich food from the list. Write it here:

_____

Chapter 14: Staying Active with Chronic Illness

Movement is possible—and powerful—even with chronic illness. Walking, stretching, low-impact exercise, and pacing yourself can strengthen your body and reduce stress. Listening to your body, staying hydrated, and avoiding extremes are keys to moving safely.

"Warrior Walks"—daily time with God through gentle walking—remind us that activity can be worship as well as wellness.

Here are some practical tips to help you stay active safely:

1. Warm Up and Cool Down Properly

Why? A proper warm-up and cool-down routine helps prepare your muscles, joints, and heart for activity, reducing the risk of injury and easing the transition between rest and exercise.

Tip: Start each workout with 5-10 minutes of gentle warm-up (e.g., light walking or dynamic stretching). Finish with 5-10 minutes of cool-down exercises, focusing on deep breathing and static stretching to improve flexibility and recovery.

2. Listen to Your Body

Why? People with sickle cell anemia can experience unpredictable pain crises, so it's essential to be mindful of your body's signals.

Tip: If you feel lightheaded, dizzy, or experience any pain, stop immediately and rest. It's better to take breaks and pace yourself rather than push through discomfort.

3. Low-Impact Exercise

Why? High-impact exercises (e.g., running or heavy lifting) can be too intense, especially during a crisis or if you're not used to vigorous physical activity. Low-impact exercises are gentler on the joints and muscles while still improving fitness.

Tip: Try exercises like walking, cycling, swimming, or using an elliptical machine. These activities promote cardiovascular health and flexibility without putting excessive strain on your body.

4. Stay Hydrated

Why? Dehydration can increase the likelihood of a sickle cell crisis, so it's critical to drink plenty of water before, during, and after exercise to keep your blood cells hydrated and flowing.

Tip: Drink water throughout the day and aim for 8-10 cups, adjusting based on activity level and climate conditions. Consider electrolyte drinks if you're sweating heavily but avoid those with excessive sugar.

5. Focus on Gentle Strength Training

Why? Strengthening muscles helps improve circulation and overall endurance. However, heavy lifting can be risky if you don't use proper form or are at risk of overexertion.

Tip: Focus on light to moderate weights with higher repetitions (e.g., 12-15 reps). Bodyweight exercises like squats, lunges, push-ups, and planks are also great options. These can be done safely and effectively to build strength and endurance over time.

6. Stretching and Flexibility

Why? Stretching helps improve blood flow, reduce muscle stiffness, and prevent injury. It's especially important for people with sickle cell anemia, as stiffness can be a common issue.

Tip: Incorporate yoga or gentle stretching into your routine. Focus on flexibility, breathing, and relaxation techniques. Consider poses that open the hips, stretch the back, and relieve tension in the shoulders.

7. Pacing and Rest

Why? Overexertion can trigger a crisis or cause excessive fatigue. It's important to pace yourself and take adequate rest breaks to avoid overloading your body.

Tip: Break your workout into smaller, manageable sessions, such as 10-15 minutes of activity followed by a rest period. Gradually build intensity and duration over time as your body adapts.

8. Avoid Extreme Temperatures

Why? Both extreme heat and cold can trigger a sickle cell crisis by affecting blood flow and oxygen delivery to cells.

Tip: Avoid exercising in extreme temperatures. On hot days, try early morning or late evening workouts when it's cooler. In winter, wear layers to protect against cold. If you're working out outdoors, be mindful of the weather and adjust your routine accordingly.

9. Focus on Cardiovascular Health

Why? Regular cardiovascular exercise helps improve circulation, oxygen delivery to tissues, and overall heart health, which is beneficial for people with sickle cell anemia.

Tip: Start with low-impact cardio activities, such as brisk walking, cycling, or swimming. Gradually increase the intensity as your fitness improves but always stay within a comfortable range.

10. Work with a Trainer or Physical Therapist

Why? Working with a trained professional can help you design an exercise plan that suits your fitness level and takes into account your unique health needs.

Tip: If possible, consult a physical therapist or personal trainer with experience in chronic conditions to help you build a safe and effective exercise routine tailored to your needs.

Stretching

Gentle stretching can be very beneficial for women with chronic illnesses, especially to improve mobility, reduce stiffness, and support mental well-being. These stretches are low-impact and adaptable to most energy levels and conditions such as fibromyalgia, lupus, chronic fatigue syndrome, or arthritis.

Important:

Always consult with a healthcare provider before starting a new exercise routine, especially with a chronic condition.

1. Neck Stretch (Seated or Standing)

- How: Gently tilt your head to one side (ear toward shoulder), hold for 10–15 seconds. Repeat on the other side.
- Why: Reduces tension and stiffness in the neck and shoulders.

2. Shoulder Rolls (Seated or Standing)

- How: Roll your shoulders slowly backward in a circular motion 5–10 times, then forward.
- Why: Helps relieve tension and improve circulation in the upper body.

3. Seated Cat-Cow Stretch

- How: Sit on a chair, hands on your knees. Arch your back and look up (cow), then round your spine and tuck your chin (cat). Repeat 5–10 times.
- Why: Promotes spinal flexibility and helps ease back pain.

4. Wrist and Finger Stretch

- How: Extend one arm out, palm up, and gently pull back on the fingers with the other hand. Hold 10 seconds. Switch hands.
- Why: Eases stiffness from joint issues or long periods of rest.

5. Gentle Seated Forward Bend

- How: Sit on a chair with feet flat. Slowly bend forward over your legs, letting your arms hang. Breathe deeply and hold for 10–20 seconds.
- Why: Helps relax the lower back and calm the nervous system.

6. Reclined Knee-to-Chest Stretch (if able to lie down)

- How: Lie on your back, pull one knee to your chest while keeping the other leg bent or straight. Hold 10–20 seconds. Switch sides.

- Why: Relieves lower back tension and stretches the hips gently.

7. Ankle Circles (Seated or Lying Down)

- How: Rotate each ankle slowly in circles, 10 times each direction.
- Why: Supports circulation and prevents stiffness, especially if you're sedentary.

Exercise Routine for Beginners:

Important: Always consult with a healthcare provider before starting a new exercise routine, especially with a chronic condition.

Day 1: Full Body Circuit (Low-Impact)

- Warm-up: 5 minutes of walking or light cycling
- Bodyweight squats: 2 sets of 12-15 reps
- Modified push-ups (knees on the ground): 2 sets of 10-12 reps
- Step-ups (using a low step or platform): 2 sets of 10 reps per leg
- Glute bridges: 2 sets of 12-15 reps
- Cool-down: 5 minutes of stretching or yoga poses

Day 2: Active Recovery (Low-Impact)

- Walking or swimming: 20-30 minutes at a gentle pace
- Stretching or yoga: 15-20 minutes focusing on flexibility and relaxation

Day 3: Upper Body Strength (Light Weights)

- Warm-up: 5 minutes of light cardio (walking, cycling)
- Dumbbell chest press: 2 sets of 12 reps
- Dumbbell rows: 2 sets of 12 reps
- Dumbbell shoulder press: 2 sets of 12 reps
- Cool-down: 5 minutes of stretching

Day 4: Cardio (Low-Impact)

- Brisk walking or cycling: 20-30 minutes at a comfortable pace
- Cool-down: 5 minutes of stretching

Day 5: Flexibility & Core Work

- Warm-up: 5 minutes of light cardio
- Planks (modified if needed): 2 sets of 20-30 seconds
- Bird-dog exercise: 2 sets of 10 reps per side
- Gentle stretching or yoga: 15-20 minutes focusing on flexibility

Day 6: Active Recovery

- Swimming, walking, or gentle cycling: 20-30 minutes
- Cool-down and stretching: 5-10 minutes

Day 7: Rest Day

Tips to Stay Safe:

- Avoid high-intensity exercise during times when you're feeling unwell, dehydrated, or fatigued.

- Consider using a fitness tracker to monitor your heart rate and ensure you're staying within a safe range during exercise.
- Work closely with your healthcare provider to ensure that your exercise routine is safe and tailored to your specific needs.

By following these guidelines, you can stay active, build strength, and improve your fitness while reducing the risk of triggering a sickle cell crisis or injury.

Remember to always go at your own pace, listen to your body, and adjust your activities as needed.

Reflection | Affirmation | Prayer | Action
Staying Active with Chronic Illness

Reflection

1. What type of movement feels joyful and safe for my body today?
2. Do I allow myself to rest without guilt when my body asks for it?

Affirmation

"My body is strong and wise. Every step, stretch, or breath is progress—not perfection."

Prayer

Father, thank You for the gift of movement. Remind me to honor my limits and celebrate my abilities. May every walk, stretch, or exercise be an act of worship to You. Amen.

Action

This week, commit to one gentle activity (walk, stretch, or strength exercise).

Write it here: _____

Chapter 15: Mind-Body Tools: Yoga, Meditation, and Breathing

Mind-body practices—such as yoga, meditation, and breathing techniques—offer gentle, accessible ways to manage physical symptoms while nurturing emotional and mental well-being.

Whether you're seeking relief from pain, a way to manage anxiety, or simply a few minutes of peace in your day, these practices are here to support your whole self—mind, body, and soul.

Yoga, meditation, and breathing are tools that calm the nervous system, reduce pain, and restore peace. They can be adapted to any energy level. Whether through child's pose, a body scan, or deep belly breathing—these practices help you reconnect with yourself and with God's presence in stillness.

Yoga Poses for Chronic Pain Relief and Stress Reduction

1. Child's Pose (Balasana)

Benefits: Gently stretches the back, relieves tension, and promotes relaxation. This pose is a great rest for the body and mind.

Instructions:

- Start on your hands and knees, keeping your knees slightly apart.
- Slowly lower your hips toward your heels while extending your arms forward.

- Rest your forehead on the mat and breathe deeply.
- Hold for 1-5 minutes, allowing your body to fully relax into the stretch.

2. Cat-Cow Pose (Marjaryasana-Bitilasana)

Benefits: Helps to improve flexibility and mobility in the spine and can ease lower back pain. Also helps with emotional release by moving through different body positions.

Instructions:

- Begin on your hands and knees, with your wrists under your shoulders and knees under your hips.
- Inhale as you arch your back, lift your chest, and look slightly up (Cow Pose).
- Exhale as you round your spine, drop your head toward your chest, and tuck your pelvis (Cat Pose).
- Continue to flow between these two positions for 1-2 minutes, moving with your breath.

3. Seated Forward Fold (Paschimottanasana)

Benefits: Stretches the hamstrings, calms the nervous system, and helps relieve anxiety and stress. It can be helpful for people who experience tightness or discomfort in their lower body.

Instructions:

- Sit with your legs extended straight in front of you.
- Inhale, lengthen your spine, and as you exhale, slowly hinge at your hips to fold forward, reaching for your feet or shins.
- Keep your neck relaxed and focus on lengthening your spine.

- Hold for 1-3 minutes, breathing deeply.

4. Legs Up the Wall Pose (Viparita Karani)

Benefits: Relieves lower back pain, reduces swelling, and calms the nervous system. Excellent for relaxation and relieving stress or tension.

Instructions:

- Sit with one hip against a wall, then gently swing your legs up the wall while lowering your back onto the floor.
- Adjust so that your legs are straight and resting against the wall, and your arms are relaxed at your sides.
- Stay here for 5-15 minutes, breathing deeply and allowing your body to relax completely.

5. Gentle Twists (Supta Matsyendrasana)

Benefits: Improves flexibility in the spine, relieves tension in the back and shoulders, and stimulates digestion.

Instructions:

- Lie on your back with your knees bent and feet flat on the floor.
- Drop your knees to one side while keeping your shoulders on the floor.
- Extend your arms out to either side, palms facing down, and turn your head in the opposite direction.
- Hold for 1-3 minutes on each side, breathing deeply.

Meditation Techniques for Chronic Illness and Stress Relief

1. Body Scan Meditation

Benefits: Increases awareness of physical sensations, helps release tension, and cultivates relaxation.

Instructions:

- Lie down or sit in a comfortable position.
- Close your eyes and take a few deep breaths to center yourself.
- Begin by focusing on your feet, noticing any sensations such as warmth, tension, or relaxation.
- Slowly work your way up your body, paying attention to each area, and consciously release any tension you may feel.
- Continue for 10-20 minutes, moving through each part of the body with mindful awareness.

2. Loving-Kindness Meditation (Metta Meditation)

Benefits: Fosters self-compassion, reduces negative thinking patterns, and promotes emotional healing.

Instructions:

- Sit comfortably with your eyes closed.
- Begin by focusing on your breath and finding a sense of calm.
- Silently repeat the following phrases, either mentally or out loud:
- "May I be happy.
- May I be healthy.
- May I be safe.

- May I live with ease."
- Once you feel calm, extend these wishes to others in your life, such as family, friends, and even strangers, with similar phrases.
- Continue for 10-15 minutes, offering compassion to yourself and others.

3. Guided Visualization Meditation

Benefits: Helps reduce pain perception, improves relaxation, and promotes a sense of peace.

Instructions:

- Sit or lie in a comfortable position and close your eyes.
- Take a few deep breaths to relax.
- Imagine yourself in a peaceful and healing environment- this could be a beautiful beach, a calm forest, or a place that makes you feel safe and happy.
- Visualize yourself breathing in healing energy from this place and sending it throughout your body.
- As you breathe, see any discomfort or pain leaving your body and being replaced with warmth and peace.
- Continue this visualization for 10-20 minutes, focusing on the healing process.

Breathing Techniques for Pain Management and Relaxation

1. Diaphragmatic Breathing (Deep Belly Breathing)

Benefits: Calms the nervous system, reduces stress, and helps control pain by improving oxygen flow to the body.

Instructions:

- Sit or lie down in a comfortable position.
- Place one hand on your chest and the other on your belly.
- Inhale deeply through your nose, allowing your diaphragm (the area just below your rib cage) to expand.
- Exhale slowly through your mouth, letting your belly soften.
- Focus on the rise and fall of your belly as you breathe deeply.
- Continue for 5-10 minutes.

2. Alternate Nostril Breathing (Nadi Shodhana)

Benefits: Balances the energy in the body, calms the mind, and reduces stress. This technique also helps clear the nasal passages and promotes a sense of calm.

Instructions:

- Sit comfortably with your spine tall and your shoulders relaxed.
- Use your right thumb to close your right nostril.
- Inhale deeply through your left nostril.
- Close your left nostril with your right ring finger and release your right nostril.

- Exhale through the right nostril.
- Inhale through the right nostril, then close it with your right thumb.
- Exhale through the left nostril.
- Continue for 5-10 minutes, focusing on the breath and the rhythm of the practice.

3. 4-7-8 Breathing Technique

Benefits: Reduces anxiety and promotes relaxation by slowing the breath and calming the nervous system.

Instructions:

- Sit in a comfortable position and close your eyes.
- Inhale quietly through your nose for a count of 4.
- Hold your breath for a count of 7.
- Exhale completely and audibly through your mouth for a count of 8.
- Repeat this cycle 4 times to start, gradually increasing as you become more comfortable.

These yoga poses, meditation practices and breathing techniques, can be powerful tools for managing pain, reducing stress, and improving overall well-being for individuals living with chronic illnesses. They are gentle and accessible practices that can be adapted to any level of experience or energy.

Reflection | Affirmation | Prayer | Action
Mind-Body Tools

Reflection
1. Which practice—yoga, meditation, or breathing—feels most approachable for me today?
2. What thoughts or emotions do I notice when I slow down and breathe deeply?

Affirmation
"I am safe, I am calm, I am whole. My breath anchors me in God's peace."

Prayer
Lord, quiet my racing thoughts and ease my body's tension. Help me rest in Your presence as I breathe, stretch, and meditate on Your goodness. Amen.

Action
Try one breathing or meditation practice for 5 minutes today. Circle which:

☐ Deep Belly Breathing ☐ 4-7-8 Breathing ☐ Body Scan ☐ Visualization

Chapter 16: Self-Care–Hair, Skin, and Nail Health

Self-care for hair, skin, and nails is about protection, nourishment, and consistency—especially for women with sickle cell anemia. Protective hairstyles, moisturizing routines, gentle products, hydration, and mindful pampering can strengthen both body and spirit.

"True beauty care is not vanity—it's stewardship of the body God gave you".

Over time, I've developed a practical, low-stress approach to hair, skin, and nail care that's gentle, effective, and especially mindful of the needs of women of color.

Hair Care: Protect, Wrap, and Leave It Alone

There's a saying that if you leave something unattended, it grows into chaos. But when it comes to hair, sometimes the opposite is true: if you leave it alone (after caring for it properly), it can thrive.

I've learned that after completing my hair regimen—cleansing, conditioning, moisturizing, and styling—it's best to put my hair away.

This is also helpful in reducing the frequency of which you have to style your hair. I wrap it up and I don't touch it unless I need to. If I'm staying home, my hair stays in a wrap or bonnet all day. This reduces manipulation, which can lead to breakage, especially in textured hair types.

Tips for Natural and Protective Hair Care:

Always moisturize before protective styling. I use something called the LOC method followed by mini twist braids. This is a great protective style because you still have access to your scalp for washing and if you wear wigs they can easily be placed under a wig cap.

What Is the LOC Method?

The LOC method is a popular hair care technique designed to maximize moisture retention in natural, curly, and coily hair types. "LOC" stands for Liquid, Oil, and Cream, representing the specific order in which these products are applied to the hair.

The LOC method involves layering products in the following sequence:

- Liquid: Start with a water-based product, such as a leave-in conditioner or plain water, to hydrate the hair and open the cuticles.
- Oil: Apply an oil (e.g., jojoba, olive, or castor oil) to seal in the moisture from the liquid.
- Cream: Finish with a cream or butter to provide additional moisture and further seal the hair, preventing dryness and frizz.

This method is particularly effective for high-porosity hair, which tends to absorb moisture quickly but also loses it just as fast.

By layering these products in the LOC order, the hair can better retain hydration, leading to softer, shinier, and more manageable curls.

LOC vs. LCO: Which Is Right for You?

While the LOC method is beneficial for high-porosity hair, individuals with low-porosity hair—where the hair cuticle is more tightly closed, making it difficult for moisture to penetrate—may find better results with the LCO method.

In the LCO method, the order is: Liquid → Cream → Oil. This sequence allows the cream to help open the cuticle slightly, enabling better moisture absorption before sealing it with oil.

Tips for Effective Moisturization

- Product Selection: Choose products suited to your hair's porosity and texture. For instance, thicker creams and heavier oils are often better for high-porosity hair, while lighter products may be more appropriate for low-porosity hair.
- Application Method: Apply products to damp hair in sections to ensure even distribution.
- Night Care: Use satin or silk scarves, bonnets, or pillowcases to reduce friction and prevent moisture loss while sleeping.

In summary, the LOC method is a strategic approach to layering products that helps natural hair retain moisture, reducing dryness and enhancing overall hair health.

Understanding your hair's porosity and selecting the appropriate method (LOC or LCO) can lead to more effective moisturizing and styling results.

Heat Styling

I limit heat styling and opt for low-tension hairstyles to protect my hair—especially important while managing chronic illness, when energy and mobility might be limited. When I straighten my hair, I take extra care since it's even more fragile in this state. I use the chase method for flat ironing and apply heat responsibly to minimize damage.

The chase method is a hair-straightening technique used with a flat iron and a fine-tooth comb (often a rat-tail or heat-resistant comb) to achieve a smoother, straighter finish with less heat damage.

How the Chase Method Works:

1. Section the Hair: Divide hair into manageable sections.

2. Comb and Flat Iron Together:

- Place a fine-tooth comb at the root of a small section.
- Follow the comb closely with the flat iron as you move down the hair shaft.
- The comb "chases" the flat iron (or vice versa), keeping the strands separated and detangled as heat is applied.

Benefits:

- Results in sleeker, straighter hair with fewer passes of the flat iron.
- Helps distribute heat evenly.
- Reduces frizz and flyaways.
- Lessens heat damage by minimizing repeated passes.

After styling, I make sure to wrap my hair properly every night to prevent breakage and split ends. A light application of hair oil can help seal in moisture and add shine. One of my go-to oils is argan oil—it's lightweight, nourishing, and won't weigh down straightened hair.

For curlier or coarser textures, castor oil or shea oil may be better suited in their natural state, but they can feel too heavy on straightened hair.

As a general rule: the heavier the oil, the heavier it will feel on your scalp, so choose accordingly based on your hair texture and styling.

Even with straightened hair, it's essential to keep your scalp clean and moisturized—especially if you struggle with dryness or flakes.

Chronic conditions can impact skin and scalp health, so being consistent with your scalp care is just as important as maintaining your strands.

I always use satin or silk scarves, bonnets, or pillowcases. I always keep a satin pillowcase on my bed—it's beneficial for both hair and skin health, and it's a great backup if I ever forget to put on my bonnet.

Nail and Hand Care: Clean, Sanitize, and Protect

Strong, healthy nails start with clean habits. I focus on maintaining clean hands and nails—right up to the elbows. I wash and moisturize my hands multiple times a day, especially because sickle cell can leave skin prone to dryness.

Nail Care Routine:
- Regular trimming and filing to avoid snags and breaks.

- Apply a nail hardener or topcoat after maintenance.
- Once a month, I treat myself to an acrylic overlay at my local nail spa—it's both beauty and self-care.

Don't neglect your feet: soak them regularly, scrub with a pumice stone, and follow up with Vaseline and socks overnight for baby-soft results.

Skin Care: Try, Test, and Tailor

Your skin is as unique as your health journey. What works for someone else may not work for you, and that's okay. I encourage experimenting with sample sizes, using coupons, and sharing unused products with friends if they don't suit your skin.

Skin Tips:

- Stay hydrated—inside and out. Drink water and use a good moisturizer.
- Be mindful of ingredients, especially with sensitive or dry skin due to medication or anemia.
- Sunscreen is a must, even for darker skin tones.

Caring for hair, skin, and nails while managing a chronic illness like sickle cell anemia is about consistency, protection, and a little indulgence.

It's about choosing routines that make you feel good and keep you healthy—because you deserve that kind of care every day.

Below are some of the best natural products to help with dry skin, dry feet, and hair/skin/nail health for those with sickle cell anemia or other chronic illness:

1. Shea Butter

Why? Shea butter is rich in fatty acids and vitamins A, E, and F, which help to deeply moisturize and nourish the skin. It also has anti-inflammatory and healing properties.

How to Use: Apply to dry skin, feet, and nails as a hydrating moisturizer. It's especially effective after a warm bath or shower.

2. Coconut Oil

Why? Coconut oil is an excellent natural moisturizer that helps lock in moisture and promote healing. It also contains lauric acid, which has antimicrobial properties, making it great for protecting dry or cracked skin.

How to Use: Massage into the skin or feet before bed or use it as a hair mask to hydrate the scalp and hair. You can also use it on cuticles and nails for nourishment.

3. Aloe Vera

Why? Aloe vera has soothing and cooling properties, making it perfect for dry or irritated skin. It's a great option for eczema-prone skin, often associated with chronic conditions. It also contains antioxidants and vitamins that can help heal the skin.

How to Use: Apply aloe vera gel directly from the plant or use an organic aloe vera gel to moisturize skin. For feet, apply after a warm soak to help soothe dryness and cracks.

4. Jojoba Oil

Why? Jojoba oil is similar to the natural oils produced by our skin, which makes it a great moisturizer that won't clog pores. It also has anti-inflammatory properties, which can be helpful for any skin irritation.

How to Use: Use as a facial moisturizer, for dry feet, or as a scalp massage oil to help nourish both skin and hair. It can also be massaged into nails and cuticles.

5. Olive Oil

Why? Olive oil is rich in antioxidants, vitamin E, and healthy fats, making it an excellent choice for dry skin and hair health. It helps to restore moisture to the skin and can prevent further dehydration.

How to Use: Use as a skin moisturizer, and as a nourishing hair oil to reduce dryness. It also works well on cracked or dry feet. For nails, rub a small amount into the cuticles for hydration.

6. Castor Oil

Why? Castor oil is known for its rich composition of fatty acids and antioxidants, which helps to hydrate and improve the elasticity of the skin. It's also known for promoting hair and nail health.

How to Use: Apply castor oil to dry skin areas or cracked feet to lock in moisture. For hair, use it as a scalp treatment to reduce dryness and promote growth.

7. Vitamin E Oil

Why? Vitamin E is a powerful antioxidant that helps to hydrate, heal, and repair dry or damaged skin. It's often used to help with scarring or to reduce signs of skin irritation.

How to Use: Apply Vitamin E oil directly to dry patches of skin, cracked heels, or rough cuticles. It also works well for dry lips or hair ends.

8. Argan Oil

Why? Argan oil is rich in essential fatty acids and antioxidants that help hydrate skin, reduce inflammation, and improve hair elasticity. It's often used to combat dry, frizzy hair and brittle nails.

How to Use: Use as a hair serum to reduce frizz or apply to the skin for hydration. For nails, massage a small amount into the cuticles and nail beds.

9. Honey

Why? Honey is a natural humectant, which means it helps draw moisture into the skin. It also has antibacterial properties, making it useful for preventing infections in dry, cracked skin or nails.

How to Use: Apply raw honey to dry skin or feet as a mask or mix with olive oil to hydrate skin. You can also use it as a hair mask to add moisture and shine.

10. Tea Tree Oil (with caution)

Why? Tea tree oil has natural antiseptic and anti-inflammatory properties, which can be useful for treating irritated, dry, or cracked skin. However, it should be used in moderation and always diluted with a carrier oil.

How to Use: Dilute tea tree oil in a carrier oil (like coconut or jojoba oil) and apply to cracked feet or rough patches of skin. You can also use it on the scalp if dandruff is an issue.

Additional Tips for Healthy Skin, Hair, and Nails

1. Stay Hydrated

Dehydration can exacerbate dry skin and hair. Aim to drink 8-10 glasses of water a day, especially when physically active, to keep your body and skin hydrated.

2. Exfoliate Regularly

Use a gentle exfoliating scrub (e.g., sugar scrub, oatmeal, or a soft exfoliating mitt) to remove dead skin cells and allow moisturizers to absorb better. Focus on feet, elbows, and knees.

3. Use Humidifiers

If you live in a dry climate, using a humidifier can help keep moisture in the air, which is beneficial for dry skin and hair.

4. Gentle, Non-Drying Soap

Choose mild, hydrating soaps or body washes (such as those with coconut oil, shea butter, or aloe vera) to avoid stripping natural oils from the skin.

5. Avoid Hot Water

Hot water can dry out skin and hair, so take warm showers and baths instead. After bathing, apply a moisturizer while the skin is still damp to lock in moisture.

6. Protect Feet

To help with dry, cracked feet, soak your feet in warm water with a bit of Epsom salt or olive oil for 15-20 minutes. Follow with a heavy moisturizer like shea butter and wear socks overnight to allow deep hydration.

7. Diet for Skin and Hair Health

Ensure your diet includes plenty of omega-3 fatty acids (from foods like salmon, flaxseeds, and walnuts), vitamin E (from nuts, seeds, and leafy greens), and vitamin A (from carrots, sweet potatoes, and spinach). These nutrients support healthy skin, hair, and nails.

Recommended Products (If You Prefer Store-Bought Options):

- CeraVe Moisturizing Cream (for dry, sensitive skin)

- Eucerin Advanced Repair Lotion (for very dry skin)
- Kiehl's Creme de Corps (for extra dry skin)
- Burts Bees Baby Nourishing Lotion (for sensitive skin)
- Moroccan oil Treatment (for dry, frizzy hair)
- Olaplex No. 3 Hair Perfector (for damaged hair)
- SheaMoisture Raw Shea Butter Restorative Conditioner (for curly, coily, or textured hair)
- Mielle Organics Rosemary Mint Scalp & Hair Strengthening Oil (great for hair growth and scalp health)
- The Honest Company Face + Body Lotion (gentle for babies and children with sensitive skin)
- Alafia Everyday Shea Body Lotion (ethically sourced and great for dry skin tones rich in melanin)

Note: When selecting products, always perform a patch test (especially with essential oils like tea tree oil or any new ingredient) to ensure no adverse reaction, especially if you have sensitive skin or other health conditions.

Keep in mind that consistency is key for long-term results.

Reflection | Affirmation | Prayer | Action
Self-Care – Hair, Skin, and Nail Health

Reflection

1. How do I currently show love to my hair, skin, or nails?
2. What's one small self-care habit I'd like to add (hydration, moisturizing, protective style, etc.)?

Affirmation

"I honor my body as God's temple. Caring for my hair, skin, and nails is caring for my whole self."

Prayer

Lord, thank You for my body—inside and out. Help me to care for it with love, patience, and grace. May my self-care remind me that I am fearfully and wonderfully made. Amen.

Action

This week, choose one simple act of care (extra water, deep moisturizer, protective style, or nail soak). Write it here: _____

Part IV: Everyday Wellness for Moms
🦋 Reflection | Affirmation | Prayer | Action

Reflection: Wellness Check-In

1. What's something healthy you've done lately that felt good?
2. What's one area of wellness you'd like to improve—without judgment?

Your wins matter. Your goals are valid—even small ones.

Affirmation: I Honor My Wellness, One Step at a Time

"Every act of care I give myself—no matter how small—is a declaration of worth. I deserve to feel well. I deserve to rest. I deserve to thrive. My wellness journey is not perfect, but it is powerful."

Prayer: Lord, Help Me Care for Me

Dear God,

Thank You for reminding me that my wellness matters. Not just so I can care for others—but because You care for me. Help me to release guilt, and embrace grace in how I care for my body, my mind, and my spirit.

Give me the strength to move, the peace to rest, and the wisdom to choose what nourishes me.

Even when I fall short, remind me that starting again is still progress.

May my small steps grow into strong habits, and may my life be a reflection of wholeness in You.

Amen.

Action Step: Weekly Wellness Plan
- Pick 1 goal for each day (water, walk, 10 min rest, vitamins).
- Keep your list where you'll see it daily (mirror, phone wallpaper, planner).
- Celebrate small wins—your body is listening.

Bonus Affirmations for Daily Wellness Motivation
1. "Small steps are still sacred."

2. "I choose one thing that nourishes me today."

3. "Wellness is not a luxury—it's a ministry to myself."

4. "Rest is not a reward—it's a rhythm."

5. "God delights when I care for the body He gave me."

6. "I can make space for joy, even in the middle of a storm."

Part V-A: Managing the Homefront

Chapter 17: Managing Time with Chronic Illness

Time management can feel overwhelming for any mom—but for single mothers living with a chronic illness like sickle cell disease, it can seem nearly impossible. If you're anything like me, you're not just managing a household; you're also managing your health, your children's needs, and often, your dreams.

This chapter offers practical strategies to help you balance responsibilities without sacrificing your well-being. By focusing on realistic planning, setting boundaries, and prioritizing self-care, you'll find ways to manage your time more effectively and reduce the stress that comes with juggling so many roles.

This isn't about perfection—it's about creating a rhythm that works for you. I like to think of it as "time balance" instead of "time management," because the goal isn't to do everything—it's to preserve your energy for what truly matters.

Over time, I've learned that consistency, planning, and the right tools allow me to make space for what I love, even while managing my health. Something as simple as meal prepping before treatment days has been a game changer.

The key is to experiment and build routines that fit your life. On good days, tackle what you can. On tough days, let leftovers and yesterday's clean rooms carry you through. Always remember grace and flexibility are just as important as consistency.

Time management tips tailored for moms like us—strong, resilient, and learning to thrive one day at a time.

1. Prioritize Your Health

- Listen to your body: Sickle cell anemia can cause fatigue and pain, so it's essential to prioritize rest and hydration. Build time into your schedule for naps and hydration, even if it means scaling back on other activities.
- Plan medical care: Schedule regular appointments and treatments in advance to avoid last-minute disruptions. Use reminders to ensure you don't forget these crucial appointments.

2. Set Realistic Expectations

- Be kind to yourself: Understand that you cannot do everything at once. Set achievable daily goals for yourself, balancing your health, parenting, and work.
- Delegate tasks: If possible, rely on friends, family, or neighbors for support with chores or childcare. Asking for help can reduce the pressure on you.

3. Create a Flexible Routine

- Routine with flexibility: Develop a flexible daily routine that considers both your energy levels and your child's needs. This might include structured times for meals, rest, and play, with flexibility for when you need a break.
- Use a calendar: Use a digital or physical calendar to map out important events, deadlines, and appointments. This can help you stay organized and anticipate busy days.

4. Time Blocking

- Set time blocks for tasks: Break your day into blocks of time dedicated to specific tasks (e.g., work, rest, household chores). This can help you focus on one thing at a time and avoid feeling overwhelmed.
- Allow breaks: Include breaks in your time blocks to rest, stretch, and re-energize.

5. Simplify Household Tasks

- Simplify meals: Cook in bulk on good days and freeze meals for later. This saves time on days when you're not feeling well.
- Use time-saving gadgets: Consider using slow cookers, air fryers, or other appliances that can reduce cooking time. Set a timer for household chores so you don't overexert yourself.

6. Work Smarter, Not Harder

- Delegate at work: If you're able, talk to your employer about adjusting your workload or working from home when you need to. You can also delegate tasks to coworkers or utilize assistive tools that help you work more efficiently.
- Take advantage of technology: Use apps and tools for grocery shopping, bill payments, and scheduling. This will save you time on repetitive tasks.

7. Practice Self-Care

- Mental health matters: Practicing mindfulness, meditation, or breathing exercises can help you manage stress and stay focused. Taking care of your mental health is just as important as managing physical health.

- Do what you enjoy: Set aside small moments to enjoy activities you love, whether it's reading, watching a favorite show, or talking with friends. These moments will recharge you emotionally.

8. Get Support

- Build a support network: If you have family or friends nearby, let them know how they can help, whether it's watching your child for an hour or helping with errands.
- Online resources: Join online communities of other single mothers or people with chronic illness for emotional support and practical advice.

9. Use Mindfulness for Pain Management

- Integrate pain management: Practice deep breathing, yoga, or gentle stretching to help manage the pain associated with sickle cell anemia. Using these techniques during lower-energy times can prevent pain from becoming overwhelming.

10. Plan for Unexpected Flare-Ups

- Have a plan for flare-ups: Since sickle cell anemia involves unpredictable pain episodes, it's helpful to have a plan for flare-ups—whether it's having someone on call to help with your child or setting aside a "flare-up day" when you can rest without feeling guilty.

By being organized, asking for help when needed, and taking care of yourself first, you can manage your time effectively even while living with a chronic illness and raising your children. Prioritizing rest and pacing yourself are key to long-term success in balancing work, motherhood, and your health.

🦬 Pause & Reflect

Managing Time with Chronic Illness

- Where are you spending time on things that don't truly matter?
- What one small rhythm could free up energy this week—meal prepping, time-blocking, or asking for help?
- What would "time balance" look like for your real life right now?

Chapter 18: Housekeeping with Chronic Fatigue

I jokingly call my approach to home care "Ghetto-OCD." I made it up, but here's what it means:

Ghetto-OCD (noun): A resourceful approach to cleanliness and organization developed as a coping mechanism—characterized by creative problem-solving, repurposing everyday items, and a deep desire to maintain a clean, comforting home environment despite limited resources or fluctuating health.

Growing up, we didn't have much—no dishwasher, no garbage disposal, no gloves. So, I learned to repurpose grocery bags, improvise, and get scrappy to keep things clean. Cleaning became my therapy, my way of creating control when life felt chaotic with sickle cell crises and a big family.

As an adult, I still carry this mindset. My home isn't magazine-perfect, but it's clean, functional, and filled with peace. God always blesses stewardship—when we do our best with what we have, He multiplies it.

This chapter gives practical tips—like breaking tasks into chunks, using ergonomic tools, creating cleaning schedules, minimizing clutter, and asking for help when needed. Above all, it's about finding comfort and dignity in your space, no matter your energy level.

Here are some helpful housekeeping tips to make the process easier and more manageable:

1. Break Tasks into Smaller Chunks

- Tip: Instead of doing everything in one go, break down your chores into smaller tasks. For example, you can focus on just one room or one task at a time (e.g., dusting one section, vacuuming one area).
- Why: This prevents burnout and reduces the physical strain. You can also pace yourself throughout the day to avoid overexertion.

2. Create a Cleaning Schedule

- Tip: Plan and organize your chores by creating a simple cleaning schedule that spreads tasks across the week. For example, clean the bathroom on Mondays, the kitchen on Tuesdays, etc.
- Why: This reduces the amount of cleaning you have to do in a single day and helps you manage energy levels more efficiently.

3. Use Ergonomic Tools

- Tip: Invest in cleaning tools that are easier on your body, like a lightweight vacuum, extendable dusters, or a long-handled mop. Ergonomic handles or tools with soft grips can reduce strain.
- Why: These tools can minimize bending, stretching, or lifting, which may exacerbate pain or fatigue.

4. Ask for Help or Use Professional Services

- Tip: If possible, get help from family, friends, or a cleaning service. Some people with chronic illness find it helpful to hire cleaning professionals on a bi-weekly or monthly basis.

- Why: Enlisting help prevents overexertion and allows you to rest, which is essential for managing your health.

5. Keep a Tidy Routine

- Tip: Try to tidy up regularly to prevent mess from accumulating. Simple habits like putting things away after use or wiping down surfaces after cooking can reduce the need for deep cleaning later.
- Why: Keeping things organized and clutter-free can prevent bigger cleaning tasks from becoming overwhelming.

6. Simplify Your Home Environment

- Tip: Minimize clutter and reduce the number of items you need to clean. Organize your living space with functional storage solutions and limit the number of decorative items.
- Why: A more minimalistic environment is easier to maintain, helping you avoid the physical strain of managing too many things.

7. Set a Comfortable Temperature

- Tip: Ensure your home environment is at a comfortable temperature. Sickle cell patients, for example, are sensitive to temperature changes, so keeping your home at a moderate, consistent temperature may help.
- Why: Avoiding extremes in temperature (like excessive heat or cold) can reduce the chance of triggering a sickle cell crisis or flare-ups of other chronic conditions.

8. Use Cleaning Products with Fewer Chemicals

- Tip: Choose natural, non-toxic cleaning products, or make your own with ingredients like vinegar, baking soda, and lemon. Harsh chemicals can irritate the lungs and skin, especially if you're sensitive due to chronic illness.
- Why: Non-toxic products reduce the risk of respiratory or skin reactions and are often gentler on the body.

9. Prioritize Rest and Recovery

- Tip: Don't push yourself to clean when you're feeling fatigued or in pain. It's okay to take breaks or even skip certain tasks if you're not up to them. Listen to your body and rest as needed.
- Why: Managing your energy levels is key to long-term health. Overexertion can worsen symptoms or lead to pain flare-ups.

10. Use Laundry and Dishwashing Aids

- Tip: If standing for long periods is difficult, consider using a dishwashing rack or a sitting laundry basket. You could also opt for a hands-free or automatic dishwashing system.
- Why: Reducing the need for long-standing activities can help prevent fatigue and strain on your joints and muscles.

11. Use a Cleaning Buddy or Companion

- Tip: If possible, work alongside a trusted friend or family member when cleaning. They can help with more physically demanding tasks, like heavy lifting or reaching high places.

- Why: Having a "cleaning buddy" not only makes tasks easier but can also keep you motivated and ensure you're not overdoing it. (My kids are my cleaning buddies)

12. Invest in Adaptive Equipment

- Tip: Consider investing in adaptive equipment that makes cleaning easier, such as grabbers or reaching tools for higher places, or a robotic vacuum for floors.
- Why: These tools can help reduce the need for bending or lifting, allowing you to conserve energy for other activities.

13. Set Realistic Expectations

- Tip: Understand that some days will be more difficult than others, and it's okay to let things slide occasionally. Focus on managing your health first and foremost.
- Why: Setting realistic expectations prevents unnecessary stress and helps you maintain a positive mindset when dealing with chronic illness.

14. Stay Hydrated and Nourished

- Tip: Drinking plenty of water and eating nutrient-rich meals throughout the day can help you maintain energy and better manage symptoms of fatigue or pain.
- Why: Good hydration and nutrition are essential for maintaining energy levels, especially when you're managing a chronic illness.

By creating a more organized and efficient housekeeping routine, you can help manage the physical and mental stress associated with chronic illness. Make adjustments as needed and don't hesitate to lean on others for support when required.

Having Ghetto-OCD isn't a flaw—it's a gift. It's the determination to create peace and structure in your space, even when your body or budget makes it difficult. And I truly believe that when we make the most of what we have, God meets us where we are and provides even more.

Pause & Reflect

Housekeeping with Chronic Fatigue

- Does your home feel like a sanctuary—or a stressor?
- What's one small "cleaning rhythm" that could bring you peace this week?
- How can you release the pressure of perfection and embrace "functional peace" instead?

Chapter 19: Budgeting on a Medical Journey

Budgeting is survival when you live with chronic illness—but it's also about dignity, clarity, and peace of mind. The costs are constant: medications, copays, hospital visits, transportation, and lifestyle adjustments like special diets or home equipment.

But budgeting isn't just about numbers. It's about protecting your peace. It's about asking: Does my financial plan support both my health and my hope?

This chapter outlines practical steps—planning for medical costs, adjusting lifestyle spending, managing lost income, seeking financial support programs, and building emergency buffers.

Equally important is addressing the emotional side of budgeting. Money carries guilt, shame, and stress. But remember budgeting is not about perfection. It's about momentum—one small, wise step at a time.

Some things to keep in mind when budgeting on your medical journey:

1. Accounting for Medical Costs

Health Insurance & Copays

- Review your insurance plan regularly. Budget for out-of-pocket costs like premiums, co-pays, deductibles, and potential out-of-network services. Even good coverage often leaves gaps.

Medications & Treatments

- Include prescriptions, over-the-counter medicines, and any disease-modifying or specialty treatments in your budget. Sickle cell patients, for instance, may require regular pain management, blood transfusions, or medications like hydroxyurea.

Specialist Visits & Diagnostic Tests

- Chronic illnesses often mean regular lab work and specialist appointments. These should be planned for monthly or quarterly.

Emergency Care

- Keep a buffer in your budget for urgent care or emergency room visits. These situations often come unplanned but with steep financial consequences.

2. Incorporating Lifestyle Adjustments

Dietary Needs

- Nutrition plays a central role in managing chronic illness. Budget for hydration, high-quality foods, supplements, or vitamins that may not be covered by benefits but are essential to well-being.

Physical or Alternative Therapies

- Some families benefit from massage, physical therapy, acupuncture, or mental health support. Even if not covered by insurance, these services can improve quality of life and should be considered in your overall plan.

Assistive Devices

- Budget for items that support independence and comfort—whether it's mobility aids, air purifiers, orthopedic supports, or home medical equipment.

3. Managing Loss of Income & Caregiving Needs

Reduced Work Hours or Time Off

- Chronic illness can disrupt employment. Anticipate changes in income if caregiving responsibilities affect work schedules or if a family member is unable to work.

Outsourced Caregiving Support

- If caregiving can't be done solely by family, consider the cost of hiring part-time help or using respite care services. These can ease burnout and should be reflected in the budget.

4. Planning for the Long Term

Medical Emergency Fund

- Set aside funds monthly, even if it's a small amount. This provides cushion during extended hospital stays or unplanned procedures.

Disability & Financial Assistance

- Research eligibility for Social Security Disability, Medicaid waivers, or other state/federal support. These programs can fill gaps and relieve pressure on your household finances.

Future Care & Financial Planning

- Consider long-term needs such as home modifications, potential long-term care, or consultations with a financial advisor experienced in chronic illness or special needs planning.

5. Managing Non-Medical Living Costs

Home Expenses

- Budget for increased utilities (e.g., heating for joint pain, air conditioning during fevers), home comfort, or accessibility upgrades like ramps or grab bars.

Transportation

- Medical appointments add up—especially if you travel for specialty care. Track costs for gas, parking, rideshare, or public transportation and include these in your healthcare budget.

6. Seeking Support & Financial Relief

Nonprofit & Charity Aid

- Many condition-specific foundations offer assistance for bills, transportation, or treatment-related expenses. Apply early—many programs have deadlines or limited funding.

Pharmaceutical Assistance Programs

- Ask your pharmacist or provider about medication discounts, manufacturer coupons, or low-income access programs. These can dramatically reduce your prescription costs.

Tax Relief

- Keep records of medical spending. You may qualify for deductions if expenses exceed a percentage of your income. Speak with a tax professional who understands healthcare deductions.

7. Communication & Collaboration

Family Conversations

- Be open about the financial realities. When all household members understand the situation, it's easier to work as a team toward shared goals.

Professional Guidance

- Social workers, nonprofit case managers, financial counselors, or hospital billing advocates can help you navigate programs, set up payment plans, or access financial tools you didn't know existed.

The Emotional Side of Budgeting

Let's be honest: Budgeting during a medical journey can feel overwhelming. Families often carry financial stress in silence, quietly coping with guilt, fear, or uncertainty. But just as physical healing is a process, financial healing takes time and grace.

This journey is not about perfection. It's about momentum.

As you reflect and plan, speak kindly to yourself. Use affirmations to reframe how you think about money and your role in managing it:

- "I am not my bank account."
- "I am doing the best I can."
- "I am moving forward, one small step at a time."

Give yourself permission to start slow, ask for help, and adjust as needed. Your financial story is still being written—with purpose, resilience, and hope.

🦬 Reflection | Affirmation | Prayer | Action
Building a Health-Conscious Budget

"It's not about cutting corners. It's about building strength—financially and emotionally."

Reflect

1. What are your top three financial concerns related to your (or your family's) medical condition?
2. Have you planned for hidden or unpredictable costs like emergency care, dietary needs, or transportation?
3. Does your current budget support your peace of mind and physical well-being?

Affirmation: I Budget with Wisdom and Worth

"I am capable of making wise financial choices that protect my peace and support my health.

I release shame and comparison.

I budget in alignment with my real life and my real needs.

Every step I take toward financial clarity is an act of love."

Prayer: Lord, Help Me Steward My Resources

Dear God,

I bring You my finances—my fears, my needs, and my hopes. Show me how to manage what I have wisely.

Help me find the courage to make hard decisions and the clarity to prioritize well.

Protect me from financial anxiety, and lead me to resources, aid, and support I may not even know exist.

Let me walk in faith, not fear.

May my budget reflect both discipline and grace, and may it serve not just survival—but peace.

Thank You for being my Provider in every season.

Amen.

Action Plan: Create a Budget You Can Live With

1. List your monthly expenses, medical and non-medical (e.g., premiums, co-pays, transportation, food, utilities).
2. Track the last 30 days of spending. What percent went toward health-related needs?
3. Identify two areas to adjust. (Can you cancel a subscription? Apply for aid? Carpool to appointments?)
4. Set one mini goal. Choose one action to improve your budget this month. Track your progress.

Chapter 20: Managing Debt

When my health declined and I lost my job, my finances collapsed. I was drowning in debt while raising kids alone, waiting for disability approval, and trying to keep food on the table. At my lowest point, I had over $100,000 in debt and no clear way forward.

The combination was overwhelming, and life became a constant juggling act, and stress felt like my new reality.

The lack of financial planning for the unexpected nearly broke me. But through it all, I held onto my faith in God, and slowly began to create a plan to not only regain control of my finances but to rise above the debt that threatened to consume me.

Just know where there is a will, there is a way. Just start praying and planning.

As I leaned on faith and developed a practice I call Pray/Speak, Plan/Write. Pray to God and speak your needs out loud. Then write them down—your plans, ideas, solutions. Writing is both practical and healing. Over time, plans will come together for the good of you and your family.

This chapter provides debt strategies like creating budgets, negotiating bills, seeking income opportunities, using aid programs, avoiding new debt, and finding support.

But most importantly—it teaches you to rebuild your relationship with money, one prayer and one plan at a time.

Simple steps to help you get out of debt

1. Create a Budget

- Track your income and expenses: Write down all your sources of income and every expense, no matter how small. This will give you a clear picture of where your money goes.

- Cut non-essential expenses: Look for areas where you can reduce spending, like eating out, subscriptions, or entertainment. Small adjustments add up.

- Prioritize debt: Allocate as much as you can to paying off debt, starting with the highest-interest debt (the avalanche method) or the smallest debt (the snowball method), depending on which motivates you more.

2. Negotiate Your Bills

- Contact creditors: Ask for a lower interest rate, an extended payment plan, or even a settlement for less than you owe. Sometimes, creditors are willing to work with you if you're proactive.

- Lower utility costs: Look into reducing your monthly utility bills by switching to more affordable plans or finding ways to save on electricity, gas, and water.

3. Increase Your Income (Even Slightly)

- Side gigs: Look for part-time or freelance work, such as tutoring, babysitting, or gig work through platforms like Upwork or TaskRabbit.

- Sell unused items: Declutter your home and sell items you no longer need through apps like eBay, Facebook Marketplace, or Poshmark.

4. Use Assistance Programs

- Government programs: Investigate government benefits such as food stamps (SNAP), childcare assistance, Medicaid, and housing assistance programs.

- Local charities: Some organizations provide help with paying bills, buying groceries, or covering other essential needs. Check with local community centers or churches.

5. Emergency Fund

- Start small: Set aside a small amount each month for an emergency fund, even if it's just $5 to $10. Over time, having a financial cushion will prevent you from going into debt when unexpected costs arise.

- Keep it separate: Store your emergency savings in a separate account so you aren't tempted to dip into it.

6. Avoid New Debt

- Say no to new credit: It can be tempting to use credit cards or take out loans, but they will only add to your debt in the long run. Stick to a cash-only system whenever possible.

- Use budgeting apps: Tools like Mint, YNAB (You Need a Budget), or Every Dollar can help you stay organized and avoid overspending.

7. Debt Repayment Strategies

- Snowball method: Pay off your smallest debt first, then move on to the next one. This provides motivation as you see debts disappearing.

- Avalanche method: Pay off your highest-interest debt first, saving money on interest over time.

8. Find Support

- Debt support groups: Seek support from others in similar situations. There are many online forums or local groups where people share tips, experiences, and encouragement.

- Financial counseling: A nonprofit credit counseling service can offer guidance on managing debt and developing a plan to pay it off.

9. Use Coupons and Discounts

- Save on groceries: Use coupons, shop during sales, and compare prices between stores or use discount apps to reduce grocery costs.

- Look for second-hand goods: Consider purchasing used items or clothes, especially for your children, to save money.

10. Mindset Shift

- Patience is key: Getting out of debt will take time, so be patient and persistent. Celebrate small wins along the way.

- Stay focused: Keep your eyes on your goals and remember why you're doing it—your future and your child's future.

By following these steps, you'll build a stronger foundation for financial stability. It may take time, but with a strategic plan and determination, you can make progress toward becoming debt-free. Even if you are on a fixed or low income-

it can be done.

Reflection | Affirmation | Prayer | Action
Managing Debt

Reflection
- How has debt impacted your peace of mind?
- What does a debt-free future look like for you and your children?

Affirmation
"I am not my debt. I am not my mistakes. I am rebuilding my financial future with peace and purpose."

Prayer
God, give me wisdom as I face my debt. Remove fear and shame, and replace it with clarity and hope. Help me see the path forward—one step, one plan, one prayer at a time. Amen.

Action
List all your debts in one place. Choose whether to start with the smallest balance (snowball) or the highest interest rate (avalanche). Take one step this week.

Chapter 21: Grocery Shopping & Meal Prepping

Grocery shopping and meal prepping can feel like massive chores when you're balancing motherhood and chronic illness. But with planning, they can become tools for empowerment.

This chapter shares strategies for shopping smarter, prepping easier, and reducing stress: making flexible lists, simplifying recipes, using coupons, batch cooking, freezing meals, and leaning on kitchen tools. It also emphasizes anti-inflammatory nutrition, family involvement, and cost-saving hacks.

The key? Grocery and meal planning should serve you—not overwhelm you.

Let's break it down into key areas to make the process easier and more sustainable for your lifestyle.

1. Planning Your Grocery Shopping

Create a Flexible Grocery List

- Start with pantry staples (e.g., rice, beans, spices, canned goods).
- Adjust weekly based on your dietary needs (e.g., gluten-free, low-carb, dairy-free).

Simplify Recipes

- Choose meals with just 5–7 ingredients.
- Plan meals ahead of time to avoid last-minute trips or unhealthy choices.

Batch Cook

- Make large portions of meals like soups, casseroles, or grains to last several days.
- Store in portions for grab-and-go convenience.

2. Smart Grocery Shopping Tips

Use Discounts & Coupons

- Clip coupons or use apps like Ibotta, Rakuten, or store rewards.
- Shop sales and bulk deals to cut costs on frequently used items.

Choose Store Brands & In-Season Produce

- opt for generic brands—they're often made by the same manufacturers as name brands.
- Buy fruits and veggies in-season or go for frozen options for better value and shelf life.

Try Pre-Cut & Pre-Prepared Items

- Invest in time-savers like pre-chopped vegetables, frozen proteins, or precooked grains.

3. Budget-Friendly Meal Prep

Cook & Freeze

- Prepare meals in bulk and freeze leftovers for future use.
- Ideal meals for freezing include stews, chili, and stir-fries.

Use Time-Saving Appliances

- Slow cookers, Instant Pots, and rice cookers can make meal prep easier and hands-free.

- One-pot or sheet pan meals reduce both prep and cleanup time.

4. Nutrition-Focused Meal Ideas

Add Anti-Inflammatory Ingredients

- Include turmeric, ginger, leafy greens, salmon, and berries to help manage inflammation.

Boost Fiber & Healthy Fats

- Use beans, lentils, oats, avocados, nuts, and olive oil for long-lasting energy and digestion support.

5. Family-Friendly Meal Prep

Get the Kids Involved

- Let them help wash produce, stir ingredients, or assemble meals.
- Use it as an opportunity to teach basic cooking skills.

Quick & Easy Meal Ideas

- Smoothie Packs: Pre-portion fruits and greens into freezer bags for fast blending.
- Overnight Oats: Assemble breakfast the night before for an easy morning.
- Wraps/Sandwiches: Use whole wheat wraps with protein and veggies for a quick lunch or dinner.

6. Cost-Saving Strategies

Stretch Protein Sources

- Use plant-based proteins like lentils or chickpeas a few times a week.
- Add rice, pasta, or vegetables to meat dishes to extend servings.

Repurpose Leftovers

- Reinvent extras (e.g., roast chicken into tacos or sandwiches, leftover rice into stir-fry).
- Freeze extra portions for days you're low on energy.

7. Physical Tips for Easier Shopping

Conserve Energy

- Use online grocery services or curbside pickup to reduce physical strain.
- Shop during off-peak hours to avoid crowds and stress.
- Choose a smaller cart if maneuverability is a concern.

8. Time-Saving Kitchen Tools

Helpful Equipment

- Consider investing in time-saving tools like a slow cooker, Instant Pot, blender, or food processor.
- Use freezer-safe bags or airtight containers to store meals and leftovers efficiently.

9. Community Resources

Food Assistance Programs

- Explore local food banks or support programs like SNAP or WIC if you're facing food insecurity.
- Many community centers and nonprofits also offer free meal programs and cooking classes.

Grocery Shopping DOs & DON'Ts

DO:

1. Make a list before shopping—it reduces impulse buys.
2. Plan meals ahead—focus on using overlapping ingredients.
3. Shop your pantry first—use what you already have.
4. Buy in bulk only when it makes sense.
5. Compare unit prices for the best deal.
6. Use coupons and store apps.
7. Shop during off-peak hours.
8. Wear comfortable shoes and clothing.
9. Use assistive devices if needed.
10. Bring a buddy for help or support.
11. Stick to the store perimeter—where most whole foods are.
12. Consider grocery delivery or pickup.
13. Keep emergency snacks on hand.
14. Track spending while shopping.
15. Freeze leftovers for busy days.

DON'T:

1. Shop while hungry—it leads to overspending.
2. Shop without a budget.
3. Buy perishables in bulk unless you'll use them in time.
4. Overlook store brands.

5. Forget to check expiration dates.
6. Feel pressured to finish all errands in one trip.
7. Rely too heavily on convenience foods.
8. Skip reading nutrition labels—especially with dietary needs.
9. Hesitate to ask for help or accommodations.
10. Shop when exhausted or in pain.

By following these strategies, you can create a grocery and meal prep routine that supports your health, respects your time, and works with your budget.

The goal isn't perfection—it's progress and self-care through simple, sustainable choices.

🦬 Pause & Reflect

Grocery Shopping & Meal Prepping

- What part of grocery shopping or meal prep drains you most—and what part feels most doable?
- What one change could make meal prep easier this week: online delivery, batch cooking, or kid involvement?
- How can you see meals not as another burden, but as nourishment and care for your body and family?

Part V-B: Parenting and Education

Chapter 22: Thriving at Home with Littles

Mothering small children is a full-body, full-heart job. Add living with a chronic illness like sickle cell anemia, and you become more than a mom—you become a warrior every single day. This chapter is about finding balance, building grace into your daily routine, and creating practical rhythms that allow you to thrive at home with your little ones—without burning out.

You don't have to do everything. You just need to focus on what truly matters, in ways that honor your health and your heart. Let go of perfection. Embrace progress, patience, and peace.

I remember the season when I had two toddlers—one with intensive medical needs and the other still breastfeeding. At the same time, I was managing the house, homeschooling, and working. That season was overwhelming, to say the least. I got through it—but not in the healthiest way. I often ignored my own needs, pushing through out of habit and sheer determination (you know how it is).

Still, somehow, my kids never missed a doctor, dental, or eye appointment. That wasn't magic—it was planning, grit, and survival. I wore my babies while doing chores. I created systems to keep our lives organized. Their schedules were on track, even when mine wasn't. I did the best I could with what I had—and I've learned a lot since then.

Now, I want to share some of those lessons with you—simple, sustainable tips that can help you stay sane, find balance, and care for yourself while raising little ones.

Tips for Moms with Small Children

1. Create a Flexible, Low-Energy Routine

- Use simple visual charts or checklists to create a daily rhythm. It doesn't need to be strict—just predictable.
- Anchor your day around meals, naps, and quiet time. This gives your child security and helps reduce decision fatigue.
- Choose flow over schedule. Let the routine serve you, not stress you.

2. Embrace the Power of Quiet Play

- Prepare a "quiet time box" filled with books, puzzles, soft toys, or coloring pages.
- Encourage independent play from an early age. It builds their confidence and gives you space to rest.
- Rotate toys weekly to keep things fresh with minimal effort.

3. Choose Energy-Saving Parenting Tools

- Babywearing or using toddler carriers can help you stay close to your child while saving energy.
- Use a stroller or wagon—even inside the house—when you're too tired to chase them around.
- Set up a comfy spot for yourself in the play area so you can rest while still supervising.

4. Prep Smart, Not Hard

- Batch-cook and freeze meals or snacks for those high-fatigue days.
- Use kitchen tools like slow cookers or meal delivery services when needed.
- Keep a snack basket at kid-level with healthy, pre-portioned options they can grab themselves.

5. Build a Support Circle

- Say yes to help. Whether it's a grocery drop-off, a friend folding laundry, or someone watching the kids while you rest—receive it with open arms.
- Use video calls to stay connected with friends and family when outings are too much.
- Join online groups for moms managing chronic illness—you are not alone.

6. Give Yourself Permission to Rest

- Nap when your kids nap (yes, even if the dishes are still in the sink).
- Practice saying "no" to anything extra that drains you. Protect your peace.
- Rest isn't lazy—it's life-giving. It's part of how you care for your body and model healthy limits for your kids.

Your little ones don't need a perfect mom. They need a mom who shows up, loves them deeply, and teaches them—by example—how to be kind, strong, and human.

By caring for yourself, you're doing something extraordinary—not just for you, but for them too.

Pause & Reflect

Thriving at Home with Littles

- Where do you put unnecessary pressure on yourself as a mom?
- Which of the tips in this chapter feels most realistic to try this week?
- Write one way you will give yourself permission to rest this week.

Chapter 23: Navigating School with Strength

When your child heads off to school, it opens a new world—for them and for you.

As a mom living with a chronic illness, navigating this system may feel overwhelming. But with the right tools and mindset, you can create a supportive environment for your child while also caring for your health.

This chapter gives you strategies to reduce stress, advocate for your family, and maintain your energy as a school mom.

Strategies for Empowered School Moms

1. Build a Relationship with the School Early

- Introduce yourself to your child's teacher and the school nurse at the start of the year.
- Share any information relevant to your health in case of emergencies or missed pickups.
- Let them know how best to contact you (text, email, etc.).

2. Set Boundaries with Communication and Participation

- You don't have to attend every PTA meeting or field trip. Pick and choose what fits your energy.
- Consider volunteering for tasks you can do from home (like managing class group texts or helping prep materials).

- Use pre-written templates for absence notes, medication forms, or parent-teacher correspondence.

3. Plan Ahead for Low-Energy Days

- Have a backup plan for school drop-offs and pickups—neighbors, family, carpool groups.
- Create a go-to "sick day kit" with frozen meals, snacks, and activities your child can do independently after school.
- Let the teacher know if there may be days your child needs extra emotional support if you're unwell.

4. Use Tech to Your Advantage

- Sync the school calendar to your phone to track events easily.
- Use apps to help with homework reminders, class announcements, and teacher communication.
- Save time and energy with online shopping for school supplies, clothes, and even lunches.

5. Normalize the Conversation About Your Illness

- Age-appropriately explain to your child what you go through and why some days look different.
- Encourage empathy, but not worry. Kids are often more resilient than we think.
- Teach them how to ask for help when they need it—at school and at home.

6. Celebrate the Wins—Big and Small

- Whether it's getting through a full week of drop-offs or packing lunches in advance—celebrate yourself.

- Create a simple after-school routine that gives you time to reconnect and rest.

Remember: you're showing your child what strength looks like in real life. You are your family's anchor.

Even if you can't be at every event, your presence, your guidance, and your love are constant.

You are not "less than" for needing rest or support—you are a lighthouse guiding your child through life.

Shine on.

Reflection | Affirmation | Prayer | Action
Navigating School with Strength

Reflection

- What parts of school life bring you the most stress?
- How can you prepare now to make those moments lighter?

Affirmation

"I am a steady anchor for my child. My love and presence guide them, even when my energy is low."

Prayer

Lord, thank You for giving me wisdom to parent with strength and grace. Give me courage to ask for support when I need it and peace when I cannot do it all. Help me celebrate the small wins and shine Your light in my child's school journey. Amen.

Action

- Choose one school-related task you can simplify (meal prep, carpool, communication).
- Identify one person you can lean on for backup support this semester.

Chapter 24: Homeschooling with a Chronic Illness

Homeschooling can be incredibly beneficial for a parent or child living with a chronic illness, as it offers flexibility, control over the environment, and the ability to manage personal health needs while still fulfilling parenting and caregiving responsibilities.

Having homeschooled for nearly 15 years, I can confidently say that the advantages have consistently outweighed the challenges—for both me and my children.

Benefits of Homeschooling with Chronic Illness
1. Flexibility in Scheduling

- Managing Health Flare-ups: Chronic illness, such as sickle cell disease, can come with unpredictable flare-ups, fatigue, or other symptoms that might require a parent to rest, manage pain, or attend medical appointments. Homeschooling allows for a flexible schedule, enabling the parent to take breaks as needed or adjust the day's routine according to their health condition.

- Avoiding the Need for a Standard Work Schedule: Parents with chronic illness often face challenges with traditional work schedules, especially when health issues make it difficult to keep a regular job or attend a workplace every day. Homeschooling allows the parent to work at their own pace, meaning they can handle lessons or administrative tasks during times when they are feeling better and take breaks when needed.

2. A Controlled Environment

- Creating a Comfortable Space: Chronic illness can make it difficult to manage stressors in an environment that isn't tailored to the person's specific health needs. Homeschooling allows the parent to create a comfortable and calming learning space. For instance, they can adjust the temperature of the room, reduce sensory overload, or include seating and furniture that accommodates their own physical needs (such as a reclining chair for rest or proper ergonomic seating).

- Managing Exposure to Illness: Parents or children with compromised immune systems or chronic illnesses may be more vulnerable to infections or environmental triggers. Homeschooling reduces the exposure to germs and stressors that could be present in a traditional school setting, allowing the parent to focus on maintaining their health while guiding their child's learning.

3. Customizing Workload to Health Status

- Pacing the Day: A parent or child with sickle cell disease or chronic illness might experience fluctuating energy levels or periods of fatigue. Homeschooling allows them to customize the pace of the day to their health status. If the parent or child needs to rest, they can shorten lessons or take a longer break. Conversely, on days when they feel better, they can increase the pace or tackle more tasks.

- Incorporating Rest and Self-care: Homeschooling provides the opportunity for the parent to integrate their self-care routines into the daily schedule. This could include time for rest, hydration, meals, or medication management, which is essential for someone with chronic illness.

4. Reducing Stress and Mental Health Strain

- Minimizing the Stress of Time Constraints: Chronic illness can be mentally and physically exhausting and adhering to strict time constraints (such as getting up early, commuting, or completing tasks on a rigid timeline) can add to the strain. Homeschooling offers a less stressful, more relaxed environment that allows the parent to focus on their health and well-being without the pressure of maintaining a rigid schedule.

- Mental Health Benefits: A parent with a chronic illness may experience mental health challenges, such as anxiety or depression, due to their condition or the stress of managing a household and family. Homeschooling provides a more controlled environment that can help reduce external stressors and promote a better sense of mental well-being. Moreover, the opportunity to focus on a child's education while managing their health may provide a sense of purpose and accomplishment.

5. Enhanced Family Bonding

- Quality Time Together: Homeschooling allows for more time together as a family, which can be particularly meaningful when a parent is dealing with a chronic illness. The flexibility of homeschooling means that the parent can engage in teaching and caregiving simultaneously, creating opportunities for positive interactions and strengthening the parent-child relationship.

- Emotional Support for Both Parent and Child: A parent living with chronic illness may need emotional support, and homeschooling provides a chance to be more emotionally available to both the child and themselves. It allows the parent to foster a sense of stability and closeness with their child while navigating their own health challenges.

6. Better Work-Life Balance

- Balancing Responsibilities: Parents with chronic illness may find it difficult to juggle a full-time job, caregiving, and managing their health. Homeschooling provides the flexibility to balance responsibilities without being overwhelmed by external pressures. Parents can work with their children's curriculum when they have the energy, and rest, when necessary, without the constraints of work or traditional school schedules.

- Time for Medical Appointments and Care: Chronic illness often requires regular medical appointments and treatment sessions. Homeschooling allows for these appointments to be scheduled without impacting the child's education, and the parent doesn't have to worry about missing work or finding childcare during medical visits. This flexibility is essential for managing both the parent's health and the child's educational needs.

7. Empowerment and Control

- Taking Charge of Health and Education: Homeschooling gives a parent with chronic illness the ability to take control of their daily routine. They can plan their day around their own or their child's health needs and adjust the educational plan to accommodate their own physical or mental health fluctuations. Having control over both the educational environment and their own schedule can provide a sense of empowerment, which can be especially important for those who feel that chronic illness is something they have little control over.

- Reduced Pressure: Traditional schooling environments may impose pressure on both the parent and the child to meet certain expectations or standards. Homeschooling allows for a more relaxed approach where both the parent and child can work at their own pace and focus on what is most important for their family's well-being.

8. Cost Savings

- Avoiding Childcare Costs: If a parent is unable to work full-time due to chronic illness, homeschooling can save on the costs of childcare or after-school care. This can be a significant financial benefit, as it allows the parent to stay home with their child while also engaging in their educational development.

- Transportation Savings: For families who need to travel to a traditional school, homeschooling eliminates the costs and time associated with commuting. This is particularly beneficial for parents with chronic illness, as it reduces the physical strain of travel.

9. Opportunities for In-Home Support

- Incorporating Healthcare Needs into the Day: Homeschooling can include time for medication, exercise, or other health routines that are crucial for managing a chronic illness like sickle cell disease. The parent can work the child's learning schedule around medical treatments, making it easier to maintain a healthy routine while managing their health.

- Assistance from Support Networks: In some cases, a parent may have a caregiver or a family member who can assist with homeschooling duties during times when they are unwell or in need of rest. This additional support can help ensure that the child receives the education they need while allowing the parent to rest or focus on self-care.

10. Customized Learning for the Child's Needs

- Fostering Empathy and Understanding: Homeschooling provides a unique opportunity for children to understand and empathize with their parent's chronic illness. Parents can explain their health in an age-appropriate way and teach their children about responsibility, compassion, and resilience. This can help the child develop emotional intelligence and maturity.

- Fostering a Flexible Learning Environment for the Child: Just as homeschooling offers flexibility for the parent, it also allows the child to learn in a non-traditional way. This environment is well-suited for children who may need a more customized or flexible educational approach. The parent can adjust the curriculum to accommodate the child's learning pace and style, fostering a more supportive, individualized education.

Homeschooling offers many benefits for parents living with chronic illnesses. While it requires planning and support, it can bring a sense of control, empowerment, and balance between health, education, and family life.

🐾 Reflection | Affirmation | Prayer | Action
Homeschooling with a Chronic Illness

Reflection

- What excites you most about the flexibility of homeschooling?
- What feels most intimidating about it?

Affirmation

"I can create a learning environment that fits both my health and my child's needs. Our family's rhythm is enough."

Prayer

God, thank You for the gift of flexibility in homeschooling. Help me to balance rest with responsibility, and give me peace on the hard days. Show me that my presence and creativity are enough for my children. Amen.

Action

- Identify one adjustment you can make to your homeschooling rhythm to better honor your energy.
- Choose one supportive resource (curriculum, online group, co-op, or family help) to lighten your load.

Part V : Parenting & Education
🦬 Reflection | Affirmation | Prayer | Action

Reflection

- Looking back at Chapters 21–23, what season are you in right now—mothering littles, navigating school, or homeschooling?
- How does your chronic illness shape the way you parent, and how might it also be strengthening your children in ways you didn't expect?
- What lessons from this section stood out to you the most?

Affirmation

"I am the mother my children need. My strength, my wisdom, and even my limits are shaping them for good."

Prayer

Lord, thank You for equipping me to parent my children in unique and powerful ways.

Give me peace when I feel overwhelmed, rest when I am weary, and clarity when I need direction.

Remind me daily that You chose me to be their mom on purpose—and You will continue to give me what I need. Amen.

Action

- Write down one new routine, boundary, or support system you want to put in place this month.
- Share one affirmation or prayer from this section with your child (or write it on a sticky note for yourself).
- Circle a date on your calendar to pause and reflect on your progress.

Part VI: Emotional Health & Mental Well-Being

Chapter 25: Emotional & Psychological Journey

Living with sickle cell disease (SCD) is not just a physical battle—it's an emotional and psychological journey that can feel overwhelming, isolating, and deeply personal. Every day, you are managing a chronic condition that affects not only your body, but also your mind, emotions, and spirit.

The emotional toll of sickle cell can be complex and multifaceted. Between the pain crises, unpredictable flare-ups, hospital visits, and the exhaustion of daily life, it's easy to feel like you're carrying the weight of the world.

And for us moms especially—when you're not only fighting for yourself but also trying to hold it together for your children—it can feel like you're unraveling at the seams.

Everyone has stressors. But when you live with a chronic illness, even everyday challenges can become overwhelming.

Common emotional and physical triggers include:
- Overworking at your job
- Grief or the loss of a loved one
- Financial stress or uncertainty
- Menstrual cycles or hormonal fluctuations
- Relationship strain
- Sleep deprivation and fatigue

What many people don't realize is that emotional and mental stress can manifest physically.

For people with sickle cell, this stress can lead to flare-ups or pain crises, creating a vicious cycle of pain, anxiety, and exhaustion.

When the Mind Feeds the Illness

Mental and emotional pressure can weigh you down. And when your body is already dealing with pain and inflammation, stress can push it over the edge.

That's when the mental spiral often begins:

- "Why me?"
- "How can I keep going like this?"
- "What's going to happen to my family if I'm not here?"
- "Who will take care of my kids?"

These thoughts are real. And they're heavy.

Sometimes, just the fear of having another flare-up or crisis is enough to bring on anxiety. Other times, it's the isolation—feeling like no one truly understands what you're going through.

You can be surrounded by people and still feel completely alone in your struggle.

This is why emotional, and mental health cannot be ignored in your healing journey.

Here are just a few of the emotional struggles many people with sickle cell experience:

1. Chronic Pain and Emotional Toll

- Pain Crisis: One of the most significant emotional and psychological burdens is dealing with the unpredictability and intensity of sickle cell pain crises. The fear of pain, frequent hospital visits, and the inability to predict when or where the next crisis will strike can cause anxiety, depression, and stress. In some cases, the pain can be so intense and constant that it leads to feelings of helplessness or hopelessness.

- Pain Management: While pain management is a key part of treatment, it's important to acknowledge the emotional toll that chronic pain takes. Patients may feel isolated, frustrated, or discouraged by the inability to live life as they would like. The need to rely on others for care or assistance during a crisis can bring up feelings of vulnerability, and a sense of loss of independence can contribute to emotional distress.

2. Anxiety About Health and the Future

- Uncertainty: Because sickle cell disease is unpredictable, individuals often experience anxiety related to the future. The fear of not knowing when the next crisis will occur, or how severe it will be, can create a sense of constant tension and worry. This anxiety may lead to a heightened focus on their health, where every symptom or feeling might be perceived as a potential threat.

- Complications: Sickle cell disease can lead to long-term complications such as organ damage, strokes, or respiratory issues. The possibility of these complications can cause stress, particularly as people with sickle cell age and face an increased risk of chronic health problems. The uncertainty surrounding these risks can exacerbate feelings of anxiety about the future.

3. Feelings of Isolation

- Stigma and Lack of Understanding: Many people with sickle cell disease may feel isolated due to a lack of understanding from others. Sickle cell is an invisible disease, and those who don't experience it firsthand may not fully appreciate the extent of the challenges faced. This can result in feelings of loneliness and isolation, as individuals with sickle cell disease may struggle to communicate their experiences to friends, family, or coworkers.

- Social Isolation: The physical limitations of the disease (such as needing to rest during a pain crisis or avoid certain activities due to fatigue) can result in social isolation. This can be especially difficult for young people with sickle cell who may miss out on social activities or milestones like school events, parties, or vacations.

4. Depression and Emotional Exhaustion

- Chronic Illness and Depression: The ongoing nature of sickle cell disease, combined with chronic pain and frequent hospitalizations, can increase the risk of depression. Individuals may feel overwhelmed by the constant need to manage their illness or by feelings of frustration that life does not feel "normal" compared to their peers.

- Burnout: Living with a chronic illness can lead to emotional exhaustion, or burnout. The mental fatigue from constantly managing one's health, dealing with medical appointments, and facing the uncertainties of the disease can wear down a person's mental health. Over time, this can contribute to feelings of burnout, sadness, and low mood.

5. Impact on Identity and Self-Image

- Living with an Invisible Illness: Many individuals with sickle cell disease struggle with their identity, particularly in relation to their illness. Sickle cell is not always immediately visible to others, meaning people may feel pressured to appear "normal" even when they are struggling internally. This can lead to frustration when others don't understand the full extent of their condition or when they feel the need to hide their pain to avoid judgment.

- Impact on Self-Esteem: Having a chronic, unpredictable illness can negatively affect one's self-esteem. Young people with sickle cell disease, in particular, may feel different from their peers, which can lead to body image issues or a reduced sense of self-worth. Feelings of being "different" or "less than" can impact social interactions and self-confidence.

6. Grief and Loss

- Loss of Normalcy: People with sickle cell disease often experience a loss of what might be considered a "normal" life. This can be particularly difficult for children and young adults who may miss out on activities such as sports, travel, and social events because of their illness. Over time, this repeated loss of experiences can lead to feelings of grief or mourning.

- Loss of Loved Ones: Sickle cell disease can cause the early death of loved ones or fellow patients due to complications related to the disease. The loss of a friend or family member with sickle cell can amplify feelings of grief, especially since it may serve as a reminder of one's own vulnerability. The fear of one day facing similar health complications can lead to anticipatory grief.

7. Coping Mechanisms

- Emotional Resilience: Many individuals with sickle cell develop emotional resilience over time. They learn how to cope with the uncertainty and pain through various strategies, including seeking support from others, maintaining hope, and focusing on what they can control.

- Support Networks: Strong support from family, friends, and fellow sickle cell patients is essential for emotional well-being. Peer support groups, whether online or in person, allow individuals to share their experiences with others who understand. These communities can be a powerful source of comfort, emotional support, and shared coping strategies.

- Mental Health Support: Therapy, including cognitive behavioral therapy (CBT) or counseling, can help individuals with sickle cell disease develop healthy coping mechanisms for managing the psychological challenges they face. Counseling can help address issues related to anxiety, depression, and grief. Additionally, support groups specifically for sickle cell patients can be beneficial for discussing shared experiences in a safe, understanding environment.

- Mindfulness and Stress Reduction: Techniques such as mindfulness, meditation, deep breathing exercises, and relaxation practices can help individuals reduce stress and manage emotional pain. These practices can be particularly useful for managing anxiety and improving mental well-being.

8. Impact on Relationships

- Family Dynamics: The emotional toll of living with sickle cell disease can also affect family dynamics. Parents or caregivers may experience stress, anxiety, and emotional exhaustion from managing a child's illness. Siblings might feel overlooked or confused, especially when the patient receives a lot of attention during a crisis.

- Romantic Relationships: People with sickle cell disease may face challenges in romantic relationships due to the fear of pain crises, hospitalizations, or complications. There can be a fear of burdening a partner or a partner's inability to fully understand the limitations of the disease. Open communication and emotional support are key to navigating these challenges.

- Social Support: Maintaining a social network can be difficult, especially when others don't understand the limitations imposed by the disease. But strong friendships can provide emotional support, especially when they offer compassion and validation.

9. Advocacy and Empowerment

- Becoming an Advocate: Many individuals with sickle cell disease find empowerment in advocating for themselves and others with the condition. This can involve educating others about sickle cell disease, participating in support groups, or joining organizations that focus on sickle cell awareness. Advocacy can lead to a sense of purpose and control, helping individuals cope with the emotional challenges of the disease.

- Raising Awareness: As more people become educated about sickle cell disease, it can reduce stigma and increase compassion. Advocacy for better healthcare access, treatments, and research also helps patients feel that they are contributing to positive change, which can be emotionally empowering.

🦬 Pause & Reflect

Emotional & Psychological Journey

Your emotions are not a weakness—they are signals.

Take a moment to name one heavy feeling you've been carrying this week.

Then ask:

Is this mine to carry alone? If not, release it into God's hands.

Chapter 26: Coping and Thriving: What Helps

You don't have to stay in survival mode.

Here are some ways to nurture your emotional health while living with sickle cell:

1. Pray and Ground Yourself Spiritually

Prayer can be a powerful lifeline. Whether it's through faith, meditation, or affirmations, staying connected to something greater than yourself brings peace and perspective in the chaos.

2. Seek Professional Help

There is no shame in talking to a therapist or counselor. Many therapists specialize in chronic illness and trauma. A mental health professional can give you tools to process emotions, manage anxiety, and cope with uncertainty.

3. Build Your Support Circle

You weren't meant to go through this alone. Lean on your tribe—whether that's family, friends, support groups, or church members. Ask for help when you need it. Share your heart. Vulnerability invites healing.

4. Journal or Voice Note Your Emotions

Get it out. Whether you write it, record it, or speak it in prayer, expressing your emotions helps you make sense of them and release their power over you.

5. Rest Without Guilt

Rest is not a reward; it's a necessity. You are fighting a battle every single day—mentally and physically. Give yourself permission to stop, breathe, and just be.

By addressing both the physical and emotional aspects of the disease, those with sickle cell can improve their mental health and overall well-being. A holistic approach that includes emotional and psychological support is crucial for improving the lives of individuals living with sickle cell disease.

If you're reading this and nodding through tears, know this:

You are not weak.

You are not crazy.

You are not alone.

You're not broken you are brave.

You are navigating a path that requires more strength than most people will ever understand. But your life is not defined by your illness. It's defined by your faith, your resilience, and the love you continue to give—despite everything you're facing.

Protect your peace. Nurture your mind. Speak kindly to yourself. And remember, your emotional health matters just as much as your physical health. You are still whole. You are still here. And you are still thriving—even on the hard days.

Finding Support Online & in Real Life

When you're dealing with chronic illness, you need your people—the ones who get it, encourage you, and lift you when it's hard.

Online Communities:

Sickle Cell 101 (Instagram/Facebook)

Sickle Cell Mom Support Groups (Facebook)

Reddit.com/r/sicklecell

Support groups via SCDAA (Sickle Cell Disease Association of America)

In-Person Support:

Ask your local hospital or hematology clinic if they offer support groups, peer mentoring, or patient education events.

Reflection | Affirmation | Prayer | Action
Coping and Thriving: What Helps

Reflection

What helps you feel most supported—prayer, people, or rest? Which of these have you been neglecting?

Affirmation

I am not weak for needing help. I am human, and my healing is holy work.

Prayer

Lord, remind me I don't have to hold it all together. Place the right people and practices around me to lift me up when I'm weary. Amen.

Action

- Who are 3 people I can lean on emotionally when things get hard? Write them down.
- Action: Reach out to one supportive person or group this week—online or in real life.

Let yourself be seen.

Chapter 27: Stress and Sickle Cell Anemia

When I was younger my uncle Mike would give me plenty of advice. Advice I wish I had listened to sooner. I believe I asked him why he was getting married again. He replied.

"Listen here guh" (girl), if something is stressing you out, let it go, you can always get another, no matter what it is. If your job is stressing you out, get another job. If your house is stressing you out, get another house. If your wife is stressing you out, get another wife."

It was that simple.

I could have prevented many of my sickle cell crises from worsening, if I managed stress effectively and earlier. Stress from toxic relationships, infidelity, poor diet, overworking and constant overthinking all played a significant role in my health history. Learning to manage your stress level is crucial to your health journey.

Stress can have a significant impact on individuals with sickle cell anemia or other chronic illnesses. While stress affects everyone to some degree, those with chronic conditions are often more vulnerable to the negative effects of stress.

How stress can influence the body, in relation to sickle cell disease or chronic illness:

1. Triggering Pain Crises (Sickle Cell Anemia)

How it works: Stress is one of the common triggers for a sickle cell crisis, which occurs when sickle-shaped red blood cells block blood flow, leading to intense pain in affected areas (like bones, chest, or abdomen).

Why it happens: Stress activates the sympathetic nervous system, which can lead to vasoconstriction (narrowing of blood vessels). In people with sickle cell anemia, this can cause more blood flow obstruction and exacerbate the pain from the sickling of red blood cells.

2. Weakened Immune System

How it works: Chronic stress leads to an increase in the hormone cortisol, which in the short term helps the body deal with stress. However, prolonged high levels of cortisol can weaken the immune system.

Why it happens: A weakened immune system makes it harder for the body to fight off infections, which can be particularly problematic for individuals with sickle cell disease or other chronic illnesses that already require careful management of their health.

3. Dehydration and Poor Circulation

How it works: Stress can cause changes in behavior, such as forgetting to drink enough water or eating poorly. In sickle cell disease, dehydration is a major trigger for crises, as it leads to increased blood viscosity (thicker blood), making it easier for sickle cells to block blood flow.

Why it happens: Stress can also contribute to a decrease in circulation by causing blood vessels to constrict, which is particularly dangerous for sickle cell patients who already experience circulation issues due to the abnormal shape of their red blood cells.

4. Increased Risk of Inflammation

How it works: Stress stimulates the release of inflammatory molecules like cytokines in the body. Chronic inflammation is a known contributor to various health conditions, including those related to sickle cell disease.

Why it happens: In sickle cell anemia, inflammation already occurs as part of the disease process. Stress exacerbates this, potentially leading to more frequent or intense pain crises, as well as other complications.

5. Mental Health Impact

How it works: Chronic stress, anxiety, and depression can be more common in individuals with sickle cell disease or chronic illness, especially due to the ongoing physical challenges they face.

Why it happens: The constant battle with symptoms and pain, the unpredictability of crises, and the social and emotional toll of living with a chronic illness can all lead to feelings of frustration, helplessness, or even depression. This mental health burden can further exacerbate physical symptoms and reduce overall quality of life.

6. Hormonal Imbalances

How it works: Stress affects the endocrine system, leading to hormonal imbalances. This can worsen conditions like fatigue and sleep disturbances, which are already common in people with chronic illness, including sickle cell anemia.

Why it happens: Hormones like cortisol, adrenaline, and thyroid hormones can be thrown off balance due to chronic stress, making it harder for the body to maintain normal metabolic and immune functions.

7. Sleep Disturbances

How it works: Chronic stress can interfere with sleep quality, leading to insomnia or disrupted sleep patterns.

Why it happens: Poor sleep further weakens the immune system and can trigger pain crises in sickle cell anemia patients. It also impacts cognitive function and emotional health, creating a cycle of stress, poor sleep, and worsening symptoms.

Let It Go to Live

Looking back, Uncle Mike's words were more than just folksy wisdom — they were a survival strategy. Stress might not be something we can always avoid, but we can choose how we respond to it.

For those of us living with sickle cell anemia, that choice can mean the difference between managing pain and being overwhelmed by it. Stress is not just a mental weight — it has real, physical consequences. Learning to let go of what doesn't serve us, protect our peace, and listen to our bodies isn't just good advice — it's necessary for survival.

Your health may not always be in your control, but your response to stress can be.

Let it go — your life might depend on it.

Pause & Reflect

Stress and Sickle Cell Anemia

Think about one source of stress in your life that keeps showing up.

Ask yourself:

Does this give me life, or does it drain me? If it drains you, what one step can you take this week to release it—or set it down, even briefly?

Chapter 28: Stress Management and Well-Being

Stress management is crucial in managing chronic illnesses, including sickle cell anemia. By understanding how stress impacts the body and using practical tools to reduce stress, individuals can improve their quality of life and decrease the frequency of sickle cell crises or other chronic illness flare-ups.

Prioritizing self-care, building a support network, and seeking professional help when needed can make a big difference in overall health and well-being.

If you're anything like me, juggling the stresses of being a single mom while living with sickle cell anemia, especially when you're also dealing with financial struggles, surrounded by toxic people and negative influences, it can all feel incredibly overwhelming.

It requires not only physical resilience but also emotional strength. While the challenges are many, there are steps you can take to protect your mental health and reduce the strain of stress in your daily life.

Tips for managing stress and improving well-being

1. Prioritize Self-Care (Even in Small Ways)

When you're juggling chronic illness, motherhood, and the weight of difficult circumstances, self-care can often feel like an afterthought. However, it's vital for your physical and mental health. Even small acts of self-care can make a big difference.

- Start with Small Moments: If you're feeling too busy, carve out just 5-10 minutes each day for a quick self-care activity. This could be a short walk, a few minutes of deep breathing, a cup of tea, or a calming bath.

- Nourish Your Body: Eating healthy meals and staying hydrated, even with a limited budget, is essential. When you're able, try to eat balanced meals with protein, fruits, and vegetables to help with your energy levels and immune system.

- Sleep: Aim for restful sleep as much as possible. Even if it's hard to get a full 8 hours, try to focus on improving the quality of the sleep you do get by maintaining a regular sleep schedule and limiting screens before bed.

2. Set Boundaries with Toxic People (Including the Children's Father)

Dealing with toxic individuals can amplify stress, especially when you feel you have no escape. Setting healthy boundaries is crucial for your emotional well-being and will help protect you and your children from unnecessary strain.

- Define Clear Boundaries: Decide what behaviors you are no longer willing to tolerate. This could include rude comments, drama, or overstepping your parenting decisions. Politely but firmly express these boundaries, when necessary, e.g., I cannot discuss this right now or please respect my need for space.

- Limit Contact: If the children's father is consistently toxic or emotionally draining, consider limiting unnecessary interactions. This might mean using text or email for communication rather than phone calls or face-to-face meetings.

- Protect Your Children's Energy: Your children pick up on stress, so try to shield them from as much conflict as possible. When appropriate, calmly explain to them why certain interactions need to be limited or handled in a certain way.

3. Find a Support System (Even if It's Just One Person)

Being surrounded by toxic people can make you feel isolated, but a support system is critical. This can help you cope with challenges and give you a safe space to recharge.

- Reach Out for Help: Find at least one person who can support you emotionally, whether it's a friend, family member, or even a support group for single parents or individuals with sickle cell. Sometimes even an online community can provide a sense of belonging.

- Therapy or Counseling (Low-Cost Options): If possible, consider seeking therapy to help you navigate stress, anxiety, and any trauma related to toxic relationships. Many therapists offer sliding-scale fees or work through community health centers that offer free or low-cost services.

- Support Groups: Look for support groups specifically for single mothers, those with chronic illnesses, or sickle cell disease. Many groups offer free meetings or online communities where you can connect with others who understand your struggles.

4. Manage Stress Through Simple, Low-Cost Techniques

When you're living with a chronic illness and facing multiple stressors, you need to use practical methods to manage stress that don't require a lot of money or time.

- Mindfulness and Meditation: Practice mindful breathing or meditation for a few minutes each day to calm your nervous system and reduce anxiety. Apps like Insight Timer or Headspace often have free guided meditations. You can also just focus on deep, slow breathing for 5 minutes.

- Exercise and Stretching: Regular movement, even gentle stretching or walking, can help reduce stress. It doesn't have to be a full workout. Simple stretches or walking around your home or neighborhood for 10-15 minutes can release stress hormones and improve circulation.

- Journaling: Journaling can be an effective way to release emotions and clear your mind. Even writing for 5 minutes a day can help reduce mental clutter. You can jot down your feelings, what you're grateful for, or a list of things you're doing well.

5. Financial and Practical Support (Managing on a Low Income)

Living on a low income adds its own layer of stress, but there are resources available to help ease the financial strain.

- Look for Financial Assistance Programs: There are often local, state, or federal programs that provide financial help for single mothers or those with chronic illnesses. Look into assistance with food, housing, and healthcare (Medicaid, SNAP, or WIC). Community centers or churches may also offer financial help or food pantries.

- Low-Cost Health Services: Seek out free or low-cost healthcare options, such as community health clinics or support organizations for sickle cell. Some hospitals and nonprofits offer free clinics for those with chronic conditions.

- Budget-Friendly Meal Planning: Plan meals around cheap, nutritious ingredients like beans, rice, frozen vegetables, and seasonal fruits. Try to buy in bulk to save money. Some resources offer meal assistance programs or free meals for children, so it's worth exploring.
- Parenting Support Services: Look into parenting resources that help single mothers, like childcare subsidies, parenting workshops, or even after-school programs to ease the load during the evenings.

6. Focus on Your Mental Health

The mental toll of being a single mother with a chronic illness cannot be underestimated. It's crucial to focus on your emotional health to keep going.

- Therapeutic Techniques for Stress Management: Besides meditation, try techniques like progressive muscle relaxation (tense each muscle group for a few seconds, then release) or guided visualization (imagining a calm, peaceful place) to manage stress.
- Practice Gratitude: Taking time each day to reflect on the positive aspects of your life, however small, can help shift your perspective. You can keep a gratitude journal where you write down 3 things you're thankful for, which can improve mood and reduce stress.
- Positive Self-Talk: Be kind to yourself. Acknowledge that you are doing your best in tough circumstances. Affirmations like I am doing the best I can, or I am strong and capable can help reduce self-criticism.

7. Set Realistic Expectations and Embrace Imperfection

Being a mom with a chronic illness often means there are days when things don't go as planned and that's okay. Perfection isn't the goal. Setting realistic expectations for yourself can help reduce feelings of failure.

- Break Tasks into Small Steps: On tough days, break tasks down into manageable chunks. Focus on one thing at a time rather than feeling overwhelmed by everything. A checklist or timer can be helpful to structure your day.

- Celebrate Small Wins: Celebrate the little victories whether it's getting through a difficult day, managing to stay calm in a stressful moment, or finding a new coping strategy. Every step counts.

8. Ask for Help (When Possible)

Finally, don't hesitate to ask for help when you need it, whether that's for childcare, emotional support, or household chores. It's okay to lean on others, and you deserve support. Reach out to trusted friends, family members, or even local organizations that aid with single parents or people with chronic health conditions.

As a mom living with a chronic illness, it's important to prioritize your own well-being even if it feels like there's not enough time or energy for yourself. Setting boundaries, finding support, and practicing simple, affordable stress management techniques are all essential steps for surviving and thriving.

Remember that you are doing the best you can under challenging circumstances, and you deserve support, rest, and time for yourself. Stay kind to yourself and take it one step at a time.

🐾 Reflection | Affirmation | Prayer | Action
Stress Management and Well-Being

Reflection

Where in your daily routine do you feel the most tension in your body? What is your stress "signal"?

Affirmation

I am worthy of peace. Even small acts of self-care protect my mind, body, and spirit.

Prayer

God, help me honor my body and mind with rest, wisdom, and peace. Show me how to guard my heart and protect my energy without guilt. Amen.

Action

Choose one simple stress relief practice (deep breathing, journaling, stretching) to add into your daily rhythm.

Chapter 29: Setting Boundaries

Setting boundaries can be one of the most empowering and self-preserving things you can do, especially when you're managing a chronic illness like sickle cell anemia or living around toxic influences.

People will overstep for sure, and if you are already irritated you can accidentally snap at them out of pain and frustration. But since you've never clearly communicated your boundaries now there's a bigger issue.

So, boundaries are for others, yes, but boundaries are for you. To stay in check as well and have healthy relationships with others.

Setting healthy boundaries

1. Be Clear and Direct

Tip: When you set a boundary, be clear and specific about what you need. You don't need to over-explain or justify your reasons, but being direct helps others understand your limits.

Example: "I can't have conversations about this right now because it causes me stress. Let's talk later when I'm able."

2. Use I Statements

Tip: Use I statement to express your needs without sounding accusatory. This helps prevent the other person from feeling attacked and makes it easier for them to hear you.

Example: Instead of "You always put too much on me," try, "I feel overwhelmed when I have too many things to handle at once. I need space to take care of myself."

3. Learn to Say No Without Guilt

Tip: Saying no is often the most difficult part of setting boundaries. But it's essential. When you say no, you're choosing your health and well-being over unnecessary stress.

Example: If someone asks you for a favor that you don't have the time or energy for, simply say, "I'm unable to help with that right now. I need to focus on my health/family/self-care."

4. Stick to Your Boundaries (Even When It's Uncomfortable)

Tip: People may push back on your boundaries, especially if they're used to you saying yes, all the time. It's important to stay firm and consistent. If someone crosses your boundary, gently remind them of it.

Example: "I've mentioned before that I need quiet time after 9 PM. I'll need you to respect that."

5. Know Your Limits and Prioritize

Tip: Understand your physical and emotional limits. If you're feeling unwell or overwhelmed, it's okay to prioritize your health over other obligations. Setting boundaries isn't about saying no to everything; it's about making sure your most important needs are met first.

Example: If you feel like you're getting close to burnout, it's okay to say, "I need to rest and take care of myself today, so I can't attend that event or handle other responsibilities right now."

6. Set Time Limits

Tip: When dealing with toxic people or situations that can drain you, it's helpful to set time limits on interactions. This gives you an out and prevents you from becoming too emotionally exhausted.

Example: "I have 15 minutes to talk right now, and then I need to focus on something else."

7. Create Emotional Boundaries

Tip: Emotional boundaries are about protecting your heart and mind. You can't control how others behave, but you can control how much you allow their words or actions to affect you.

Example: If someone is being negative or critical, you can say, "I understand that you're upset, but I'm not able to engage in this conversation right now. Let's talk when things are calmer."

8. Seek Support from Others (If Necessary)

Tip: It can help to have someone in your corner who knows the boundaries you're trying to set. They can offer encouragement and even help you reinforce your boundaries if needed.

Example: If you're setting boundaries with your children's father or a family member, let a trusted friend or family member know what you're working on so they can offer support and help keep you accountable.

9. Respect Others Boundaries, Too

Tip: Healthy boundaries go both ways. Be sure you respect others boundaries as much as you expect them to respect yours. This mutual respect fosters healthier relationships.

Example: If someone else expresses a need for space or time for themselves, honor that without guilt or pressure to change their decision.

10. Be Prepared for Pushback

Tip: Sometimes people will react negatively to your boundaries, especially if they've been used to you giving in or overextending yourself. Stay calm and reaffirm your boundary without getting defensive.

Example: If someone challenges your decision, you can calmly respond, "I understand that you may not agree, but this is what I need right now for my health and peace of mind."

Bonus Tip: Reassess Boundaries Regularly

Your needs may change over time, and so should your boundaries. It's okay to reassess your boundaries regularly, especially as you learn more about your limits and priorities.

Example: If your circumstances change, you might need to reassess your boundaries with family or friends and adjust accordingly.

Remember boundaries are a form of self-love.

Setting boundaries isn't selfish, it's a way of protecting yourself so you can be the best version of yourself for your children and your health. It's a form of self-respect, and when you set boundaries, you are teaching others how to treat you in a healthy way.

Be proud of yourself for taking this important step and give yourself grace as you navigate the process.

🦋 Pause & Reflect

Setting Boundaries

Boundaries are not walls; they are bridges to healthier relationships.

Take a moment: where do you need to say no so you can say yes to peace?

Part VI: Emotional Health & Mental Well-Being
Reflection | Affirmation | Prayer | Action

Dear Warrior Mom

You've just read about the emotional toll of stress, chronic illness, and the importance of boundaries. Now it's time to pause and be fully present—with yourself.

This is your life, not anyone else's version of it. You are worthy of comfort, peace, and joy, regardless of your circumstances.

Reflection: Your Mental & Emotional Check-In

Take a deep breath. Reflect honestly:

- What emotions are rising in me right now?
- Which parts of my emotional journey have I kept hidden or unspoken?
- How has sickle cell (or another chronic illness) shaped my identity or self-worth?
- Who makes me feel safe, seen, and supported—and who drains or diminishes me?
- What emotion have I been carrying most often?
- What's draining me emotionally, and what's refueling me?
- Where do I need to draw a boundary—for my peace?

Finish this sentence:

"Emotionally, I am learning to let go of _____ and hold on to _____."

Affirmation: My Peace Is My Power

"I am not my illness.

I am worthy of rest, love, and healing.

I am allowed to feel, allowed to rest, and allowed to grow.

My emotions are valid, but they do not define me.

I protect my peace, honor my boundaries, and choose healing daily.

Even in struggle, I am still becoming."

Prayer: Lord, Be My Calm in the Chaos

Dear God, You see the storms I hide inside—the stress, the sorrow, the pressure to stay strong.

Calm my mind. Quiet my heart. Remind me that healing isn't just physical—it's emotional too.

Help me release guilt and embrace grace.

Teach me to set boundaries that protect my joy and clarity. Let peace be my portion and rest be my rhythm. Walk with me through every anxious moment until I can breathe again. Amen.

Action: Building Your Emotional Wellness Plan

Healing isn't about fixing everything overnight—it's about showing up for yourself, one step at a time. Choose 1–2 actions this week:

1. Emotional Outlet – Pick a safe outlet (journaling, talking, therapy, prayer, music, or movement) to release emotions.

2. Peace List – Write 3 small things that bring you calm (warm baths, a favorite song, deep breathing). Post it where you'll see it daily.
3. Daily Check-In – Set aside 10 minutes each day to pause, breathe, and note how you're feeling.
4. Write to Your Past Self – Send love and reassurance to the version of you who once carried pain.
5. Reach Out – Call or text someone you trust. Vulnerability builds connection.
6. Set 2 Boundaries – Examples: saying no when you're drained, creating tech-free hours, asking loved ones to respect your healing process.
7. Affirm Yourself – Speak the affirmation above each morning.
8. Schedule Rest – Pick one guilt-free rest day this week. Treat it like a sacred appointment with your healing.
9. Ask for Help—Then Accept It – Make a list of people or resources you can lean on this month.

Gentle Reminder

Emotional wellness isn't about always being "okay."

It's about being honest, being held, and being open to healing.

You are allowed to rest, reset, and rebuild at your own pace.

Your feelings are not too much.

Your healing is holy work.

And you, Warrior Mama, are worthy of both.

Part VII: Relationships and Family Dynamics

Chapter 30: Being Present When You're Not Well

Showing up for your kids and family when you're drained or in the middle of a sickle cell crisis is incredibly challenging.

You're balancing your own health with the needs of those you love. But presence doesn't always require perfection or energy—it simply asks for love in the ways you can give it.

Whether it's Lego-Movie Night, pizza and board games, or quiet cuddles on the couch—small traditions create memories that matter more than big trips.

Kids don't need Disneyland; they need you. Even on your hardest days, your presence can bring comfort.

Here are some tips on how to balance both:

1. Communicate Honestly with Your Kids

- Tip: Age-appropriate communication can help your children understand that you're not being distant but simply need to take care of your health.

- Example: "Mommy is feeling tired today because of my sickness, so I need to rest a bit. I still love you and will be here for you, but I need to take care of myself too."

- This can help them feel reassured and reduce any confusion or worry. It also helps to normalize the concept of self-care for them.

2. Create Simple, Low-Energy Bonding Activities

Tip: Even if you're feeling too tired to engage in your usual activities, you can still bond with your kids in low-energy ways that don't drain you.

Examples:

- Story-time: Reading a favorite book to them or letting them choose a story. You can also listen to audiobooks together.
- Cuddling and Talking: A cozy moment of physical closeness, like snuggling up on the couch, can be comforting for both you and your kids.
- Creative Play (Low-Energy): Drawing, coloring, or doing a simple puzzle can be relaxing for you and still engaging for them.
- Music and Singing: Play some calming or fun music and sing along, or even just listen to music together.

3. Set Up a Comfortable Rest Zone

Tip: Create a rest zone in your home where you can retreat to for short breaks without feeling guilty. This allows you to recharge while still being close to your kids.

Example: You can have a cozy chair or spot on the couch with pillows and a blanket where you can rest but still be in the same room, allowing you to keep an eye on them if they need you.

- You can also create a routine where your kids know it's quiet time, which gives you both rest.

4. Delegate and Ask for Help (Even if Just for a Little While)

Tip: If possible, ask for help or delegate some responsibilities to others. Whether it's a trusted friend, relative, or even older children, asking for help can give you the space you need to rest and recover.

Example: If the children's father is available, you could arrange for him to take over certain tasks for a bit, even if it's just getting the kids ready for bed or making a meal.

- You can also try setting up a family check-in routine where each family member is assigned a simple task (even kids can help with small things like tidying up or setting the table).

5. Simplify the Day's Routine

Tip: On days when you're struggling physically, simplify your family's routine as much as possible.

Example:

- Prepare simple meals (like easy-to-make sandwiches, fruit, or pre-prepped meals) to minimize cooking time and effort.

- Skip or shorten the usual routines, like reducing screen time or opting for shorter activities (e.g., 10-minute playtime rather than an hour).

- Use frozen meals or easy-to-prepare foods that can save you energy.

- Focus on core activities that ensure your family's basic needs are met, such as eating and resting.

6. Set Up Special Easy Family Time

Tip: Even when you're exhausted or unwell, you can still connect in ways that don't require a lot of energy.

Example:

- Family movie night: Make it a low-key event with a favorite movie and some popcorn.
- Snuggling during TV time: Let the kids crawl into bed or on the couch with you and watch a show, talk, or simply enjoy being together.
- Games that don't require too much effort: Something like board games, card games, or simple activities where you can play from the couch (like trivia or I Spy).

7. Practice Self-Compassion

Tip: Remind yourself that you're doing your best. If you're tired or going through a mild crisis, it's okay to take things slower and focus on quality over quantity.

Example: Instead of thinking, "I should be doing more, try reframing it as, I'm doing the best I can with what I have today. The goal is to keep stress at a manageable level, and guilt doesn't help anyone.

8. Involve Your Kids in Caregiving

Tip: If your children are old enough, involve them in caring for you in a way that's empowering for them and doesn't make you feel overwhelmed.

Example: Let them fetch a blanket for you when you're feeling cold or ask them to quietly sit with you or help with small tasks. They'll feel included and gain a sense of responsibility without you feeling like you have to do everything yourself.

9. Keep Routines Flexible

Tip: While routines are comforting for kids, being too rigid can add extra stress. Keep your daily plans flexible so that when you're struggling physically, you can adapt without feeling like you're failing.

Example: If you normally have a set bedtime, it's okay to make it earlier or later depending on how you feel. If they usually have after-school activities, it's fine to skip them or replace them with a quieter activity if you're not up to it.

10. Focus on Emotional Presence, Not Perfection

- Tip: You don't have to do everything perfectly or even do all the usual things. What matters is that you're emotionally present.
- Example: Even if you're too tired to engage in their usual activities, simply being emotionally available for your kids and giving them your full attention, even if it's for a short time, makes a big impact.

It's normal to feel torn between taking care of yourself and showing up for your family, especially if you're a single mom living with chronic illness. The key is finding ways to balance.

By prioritizing your health and finding moments of connection with your kids that are manageable for you. On your hardest days, remember that you're doing the best you can, and your kids will understand love and care in ways that don't always have to be physical or active.

It's the emotional connection and time together that matter most, even when things are tough.

🐂 Pause & Reflect

Being Present When You're Not Well

Think of one way you can be present with your family this week, even if your body needs rest.

What's one "low-energy" tradition you can begin or continue that keeps you connected?

Chapter 31: Loving Someone with Chronic Illness

Loving someone with a chronic illness requires patience, compassion, and strength. I know this intimately—through my own health, walking alongside my late sister, and caring for my son with multiple conditions. It's not easy, but love makes space for resilience.

To love well, you must both learn about the illness and listen beyond words—sometimes becoming an advocate when your loved one cannot speak for themselves. Your steady presence can be their greatest gift.

Here are a few things you can do to help:

1. Learn About the Illness

Understanding sickle cell anemia, its symptoms, and how it affects the person's life can make you more empathetic and better equipped to provide support. This helps you avoid misconceptions and be more patient during flare-ups.

2. Provide Emotional Support

Chronic illnesses can be mentally and emotionally exhausting. Sometimes, just listening and being there for them can make a big difference. You can check in regularly, encourage them to talk about how they're feeling, or simply let them know you're available if they need someone.

3. Help with Daily Tasks

Sickle cell crises or flare-ups can cause severe pain and fatigue. Offering to help with household chores, errands, or driving them to appointments can ease the burden on your loved one. Even small things like picking up groceries or helping with kids can be a big relief.

4. Be Flexible and Patient

Understand that there may be days when they need to cancel plans or take it easy. Flexibility in your expectations can help them feel less pressure. Chronic illness often has unpredictable flare-ups, so being understanding when plans change is important.

5. Encourage Healthy Habits

Offer to join them in activities that promote health, like eating nutritious meals together, going for walks, or staying hydrated. For people with sickle cell, staying hydrated and avoiding triggers (like extreme temperatures or dehydration) is really important.

6. Advocate for Them

If they're not able to, you can help advocate for their needs, whether it's at medical appointments, with employers, or in social situations. Being an advocate can sometimes make it easier for them to get the care or accommodations they need.

7. Respect Their Boundaries

People with chronic illnesses can be very specific about how they like to be supported. Some may want to talk about their condition, while others may prefer not to. Respecting their boundaries is key to maintaining a healthy relationship.

8. Encourage Social Connection

Chronic illness can sometimes lead to isolation. Encourage them to stay connected with friends and family, whether it's through phone calls, video chats, or even small gatherings that work around their health needs. Social support is a huge part of managing chronic illness.

9. Offer Financial Help if Needed

Sickle cell anemia often requires regular medical care, which can be expensive. If it's within your means, offering financial support or helping them navigate resources for assistance can ease some of their stress.

10. Be Aware of the Impact on Mental Health

Chronic illness can affect mental health too, so be mindful of signs of depression or anxiety. Encouraging them to seek professional help if needed and being there for them when they do can provide additional support.

Ultimately, your consistent presence and understanding go a long way in providing comfort.

It's all about being there, respecting their needs, and helping in ways that make their lives easier and more manageable.

🕯 Reflection | Affirmation | Prayer | Action
Loving Someone with Chronic Illness

Reflection
What's one way you can show love to someone in your life with chronic illness—without trying to "fix" them?

Affirmation
My love is strongest when it is patient, gentle, and present.

Prayer
Lord, help me love with compassion and wisdom. Teach me to listen more than I speak, and to advocate when needed without overstepping. Amen.

Action
This week, check in with a loved one who may be struggling. Ask: "How can I best support you right now?"

Chapter 32: Romance & Chronic Illness

Chronic illness brings unique challenges into romantic relationships. It can tempt you to isolate, but love thrives in vulnerability and connection. You deserve intimacy, joy, and partnership—even with sickle cell.

Strong relationships are built on honesty, flexibility, education, shared coping strategies, and boundaries. When both partners embrace empathy, intimacy can flourish in new ways, and illness becomes just one part of the story—not the whole.

In middle school, I had a close guy friend who knew about my illness. I once expressed to him that I didn't think I'd ever get married because I didn't believe anyone would want to take on the burden of a sick wife. His response was simple yet profound: "If we're older and you want to get married; I'll marry you and I'll take care of you." That promise—true friendship.

Living with sickle cell has often pushed me to isolate myself, probably just when I've needed connection the most. I've always been a homebody and find comfort in my own company. While seclusion offers a certain kind of peace and a chance to grow within myself, I've learned that truly involving myself in the lives of those who love me is a different, more powerful kind of self-care. It's medicine for the spirit.

In the face of chronic illness, there can be a temptation to retreat or assume that people won't understand. But the truth is, embracing relationships—whether romantic or platonic—is essential for healing.

Don't let your chronic illness stop you from connecting with others. Time is precious, and life is short. Make space for love in all its forms, even when you're struggling. It's vital to nurture the relationships that can uplift you when you need it most. You deserve to feel the warmth of connection, and in turn, it can provide a sense of strength and purpose that illness alone cannot.

Navigating romantic relationships while living with sickle cell anemia or other chronic illnesses can present unique challenges, but it's entirely possible to maintain a healthy, fulfilling partnership with open communication, understanding, and mutual respect.

Tips to help foster strong, supportive romantic relationships while managing chronic illness:

1. Communicate Openly and Honestly

- Be transparent about your illness: It's crucial to share with your partner what living with sickle cell or a chronic illness entails, including the symptoms, potential flare-ups, and treatments. This helps your partner understand what you're experiencing physically and emotionally, which can prevent misunderstandings.

- Discuss limitations and needs: Let your partner know if there are times when you need rest, assistance, or emotional support. Being honest about your limitations will allow your partner to be more empathetic and understanding.

- Express your emotions: Don't bottle up how you're feeling. Share both the highs and lows with your partner, including fears, frustrations, or concerns about your health, so they can better support you.

2. Set Realistic Expectations

- Acknowledge your energy levels: Chronic illness often means that your energy and physical capabilities may vary from day to day. It's important to communicate this to your partner so they don't feel neglected when you need rest or can't participate in certain activities.

- Be patient with your limitations: There may be times when you're not able to do things you used to, such as going out or engaging in certain physical activities. Being honest about your health condition can help set realistic expectations on both sides about what your relationship looks like.

3. Educate Your Partner

- Provide resources: If your partner isn't familiar with sickle cell or your specific chronic illness, take the time to educate them. Provide them with information on your condition, its impact on your life, and ways they can be supportive.

- Create understanding: The more informed your partner is about the nature of your illness, the more compassionate and supportive they can be. Encourage them to ask questions and be involved in the management of your condition.

4. Develop Coping Strategies Together

- Create a routine together: Work with your partner to establish routines that account for your health. For example, scheduling rest days, planning low-energy activities, or finding ways to stay active that work for you both can help maintain a balanced and healthy relationship.

- Build resilience: Facing the challenges of chronic illness together can strengthen your bond. Develop coping strategies that help both of you manage difficult moments -this could include relaxation techniques, mutual support during flare-ups, or simply being present for each other during challenging times.

5. Prioritize Emotional Support

- Recognize emotional needs: Chronic illness can take an emotional toll on both the person affected and their partner. It's important to support each other emotionally. Encourage open conversations about feelings of isolation, fear, or sadness.

- Practice empathy and patience: Understanding that both partners may experience frustration or grief - whether due to health limitations or emotional exhaustion -is key. Be patient with each other and work together to find solutions to any emotional struggles that arise.

- Create space for joy: Make time for fun, joy, and intimacy. Chronic illness doesn't define your entire relationship, so prioritize moments of connection and happiness.

6. Maintain Physical Intimacy

- Communicate about physical intimacy: Health conditions like sickle cell anemia can affect physical intimacy in various ways, such as fatigue or pain. Discuss what you're comfortable with and how you can maintain closeness, even if your physical capabilities change.

- Be open to adapting Intimacy can take different forms-sexual or non-sexual. Embrace the variety of ways to connect physically, from holding hands to cuddling to having open conversations about needs and desires.

- Listen to your body: Respect your body's cues regarding intimacy. If you're in pain or too fatigued, be open with your partner, and find ways to nurture the relationship that don't require physical exertion.

7. Don't Let the Illness Define the Relationship

- Focus on shared interests: Remember that your chronic illness is just one aspect of your life, and it doesn't have to define the entirety of your relationship. Spend quality time doing things you both enjoy-whether it's watching movies, cooking together, or enjoying hobbies.

- Strengthen emotional connections: While your illness is important to acknowledge, make sure the relationship focuses on emotional bonding, respect, and shared experiences. Celebrate each other's strengths, dreams, and accomplishments, and not just the challenges you face.

8. Navigate Healthcare Together

- Involve your partner in health decisions: If you're comfortable, include your partner in medical appointments or decisions related to your treatment. This can increase their understanding and involvement in your care and help them feel more empowered to support you.

- Ask for help when needed: Chronic illness sometimes requires a partner to step in as a caregiver. Don't hesitate to ask for help when you need it, but also be mindful of not overburdening your partner. Find a balance between self-care and seeking assistance.

9. Set Boundaries

- Respect each other's needs: It's important to establish boundaries, both in terms of your illness and your relationship. While your partner may want to help, they may also need time and space to care for themselves. Healthy boundaries create a supportive, rather than dependent, dynamic.

- Guard against burnout: Be mindful of both your own emotional and physical limits and those of your partner. Both of you may need breaks from caregiving roles, so it's important to create space for self-care and avoid role overload.

10. Plan for the Future Together

- Discuss long-term plans: Chronic illness may prompt you to think about the future differently. Have open conversations about long-term goals, including plans for managing your illness, family planning, and expectations for the future.

- Reframe your relationship goals: While certain plans or expectations may need to be adjusted due to chronic illness, it's important to reframe these goals and remain optimistic about your future together. Collaborate on how to build a life full of love, adventure, and shared memories, regardless of challenges.

11. Take Time for Yourself

- Preserve your independence: While a supportive partner is crucial, it's equally important to maintain a sense of independence. Focus on your personal health and hobbies, and don't feel guilty about taking time for yourself when you need it.

- Foster self-love: Maintaining your self-esteem and mental health is vital for a healthy relationship. Engage in activities that make you feel good about yourself and help you feel empowered in your relationship.

Romantic relationships when managing chronic illness can be deeply fulfilling, provided there is mutual respect, understanding, and communication. The key is creating a dynamic where both partners feel supported, understood, and connected.

By embracing vulnerability, sharing both the joys and challenges of living with chronic illness, and supporting each other's growth, couples can form a relationship that's resilient and fulfilling, regardless of the obstacles they may face. Allowing them to embrace love amidst chronic illness.

Pause & Reflect

Romance & Chronic Illness

Do you believe you are worthy of love and partnership, even with illness?

Write down one fear you carry about relationships and then reframe it as truth rooted in love.

Chapter 33: Grief, Loss and Chronic Illness

Grief is part of every life, but living with chronic illness makes grief heavier, sometimes even triggering crises.

I know this deeply—I lost my sister to our shared disease, while pregnant with my youngest child, and already stretched thin caring for a medically fragile son.

Life was truly overwhelming.

However, grief is something we all face at some point in our lives, and when living with a chronic illness like sickle cell anemia, it's even more important to have tools to navigate it.

The emotional and physical toll of chronic illness can make grief feel even more overwhelming, especially when the loss involves health, relationships, or life expectations.

Grief can't be rushed, but it can be carried with gentleness, support, and faith.

Allow yourself to feel, seek connection, honor your limits, and find healing through meaning, memory, and community.

In this chapter, I'll share some tips on managing grief while living with a chronic illness, to help you find balance and take care of yourself during one of life's toughest challenges.

Tips to help navigate grief

1. Acknowledge Your Grief and Allow Yourself to Feel

- Give yourself permission to grieve: It's essential to accept that grief is a natural and necessary part of life, and that your grief may be more complex because of your chronic illness. Whether you're grieving the loss of health, opportunities, or relationships, it's okay to feel sadness, frustration, or anger.
- Embrace your emotions: Don't suppress your feelings. Cry if you need to, or express your emotions through writing, art, or talking to someone you trust. Recognizing your emotions allows you to begin healing.

2. Seek Support from Others

- Reach out to people who understand: Lean on friends, family, or support groups who know what you're going through. Sometimes, connecting with people who share your experience (like others with sickle cell anemia or chronic illness) can help you feel less alone in your grief.
- Therapy and counseling: Professional support can be invaluable when coping with grief. A therapist experienced in working with people who have chronic illness can help you navigate complex emotions, especially if you're experiencing depression, anxiety, or prolonged grief.

3. Focus on Self-Compassion

- Practice self-care: When you're grieving, it can be easy to neglect your physical and emotional needs. Taking care of your body and mind can help you manage both

your illness and grief. Engage in activities that nurture you, such as meditation, yoga, or taking a relaxing bath.
- Be kind to yourself: Chronic illness can often bring feelings of guilt or self-blame, especially if your grief is tied to lost opportunities or the impact your illness has on others. Remind yourself that it's okay not to be perfect and that your feelings are valid.

4. Balance Physical Care with Emotional Healing

- Respect your physical limitations: Grieving while managing chronic illness can sometimes feel physically draining. Make sure to listen to your body and rest when needed. It's important to acknowledge that grief can impact your energy levels, making it harder to manage both the emotional and physical aspects of your life.
- Stay on top of medical care: Keep up with your medical treatments and appointments, even during periods of grief. Physical health and emotional well-being are interconnected, and taking care of your health can provide some stability during difficult times.

5. Practice Mindfulness and Stress-Reduction Techniques

- Mindfulness meditation: Practice mindfulness to stay present with your grief and not get overwhelmed by "what if" thoughts or worries about the future. Mindfulness can help you process emotions without judgment.
- Breathing techniques: Stress and anxiety often accompany grief. Practicing deep breathing exercises,

like diaphragmatic breathing or alternate nostril breathing, can help you ground yourself when emotions feel intense.

6. Create Meaning and Find Purpose in the Loss

- Reframe your grief: Although it's difficult, you can find meaning in your grief. For instance, if you're grieving lost health or opportunities, consider how your illness has shaped you in positive ways- perhaps giving you empathy, resilience, or a deeper appreciation for life.

- Honor the loss: Whether you've lost a loved one, your health, or something else, find a way to honor that loss. This could be through writing, creating a ritual, or simply remembering with gratitude. Giving space to the memory can help you heal.

7. Set Realistic Expectations

- Don't rush the healing process: Grief takes time, and everyone experiences it differently. Be patient with yourself, and don't feel pressured to "move on" before you're ready.

- Adjust your goals: Chronic illness may limit what you can do physically, and grief may affect your emotional energy. Reassess your goals and adjust them to a pace that's manageable for you. It's okay to take small steps toward healing instead of expecting yourself to "bounce back" quickly.

8. Reach Out to Faith or Spirituality

- Explore your spirituality: Many people find comfort in their faith or spiritual practices. Prayer, connecting with a spiritual community, or reading inspirational texts can provide solace during times of loss.

- Meditation or prayer for healing: Guided prayer or meditation focused on healing can help connect you to a sense of peace, even amidst grief.

9. Find Creative Outlets for Expression

- Art and creative expression: Writing, drawing, painting, or music can be therapeutic ways to process grief. These outlets allow you to express emotions that may feel too overwhelming to speak about.

- Journaling: Writing about your grief and your experience with illness can help you reflect on your emotions and find clarity. Journaling can also serve to document your healing journey over time.

10. Consider Grief Support Groups

- Join a grief support group: Sometimes, finding a group of people who are also navigating loss can be helpful. Support groups (in person or online) can provide emotional connection, validation, and shared wisdom for coping with both grief and chronic illness.

11. Take Time to Reflect on Positive Memories

- Remember what you've learned: As hard as it may be, reflecting on the positive memories, lessons, and growth you've experienced in the face of your illness or loss can bring comfort. It can be helpful to remember how you've persevered and the ways you've found strength in difficult times.

12. Avoid Isolation

- Stay connected: Grief can lead to withdrawal and isolation, but isolation can amplify the pain. Make an effort, even when it feels difficult, to maintain social connections. Reach out to family and friends, or consider joining support communities for chronic illness or grief.

- Small social interactions: Even if you can't engage in social activities the way you used to, small interactions with loved ones (like a text, phone call, or a quiet moment together) can remind you that you are supported and not alone.

Grieving while managing sickle cell anemia or any chronic illness is an intensely personal and complex process.

Be gentle with yourself, understanding that the grief you experience might be layered and ongoing. Over time, through support, self-compassion, and reflection, healing is possible.

Your journey may look different from others, and that's okay. What's important is embracing the healing journey and finding what works for you, taking it one day at a time, and trusting in your own resilience.

🦬 Reflection | Affirmation | Prayer | Action
Grief, Loss & Chronic Illness

Reflection

What loss are you still carrying quietly? What would it mean to give yourself permission to grieve fully?

Affirmation

My grief is real. My healing is allowed. I can carry loss and love at the same time.

Prayer

God, hold me gently in my grief. Teach me to honor my pain without being consumed by it. Help me find healing and meaning even in sorrow. Amen.

Action

Choose one small way to honor a loss this week—write a letter, light a candle, create something, or share a memory.

🦋 Part VII: Relationships and Family Dynamics- Healing in Relationship

Reflection | Affirmation | Prayer | Action

A space to reflect, reconnect, and reclaim peace in your relationships—while honoring your healing.

Reflection: Loving While Healing

Think about a relationship that has shifted—because of your illness, your growth, or your need for rest.

1. What do you miss about that relationship?
2. What do you need now—from that person or from yourself?
3. What are you proud of in how you've shown up?

Journal Prompt:

Write a letter to that person or to yourself.

Offer grace, name your truth, and let go of what no longer serves you—even if you never send it.

Affirmation: I Can Love Others and Still Choose Myself

"I can love deeply and still set boundaries.

I can care without over-carrying.

I am allowed to protect my peace and speak my needs.

Healing does not make me selfish—it makes me whole."

Prayer: God, Teach Me to Love from a Place of Wholeness

Dear God, Relationships change.

Sometimes they hurt. Sometimes they heal.

Help me to love well—even while I heal.

Give me strength to speak my needs without guilt, and courage to set boundaries without shame.

Teach me to offer grace to others, but also to myself.

Help me to forgive what I can, release what I must, and hold onto what truly nurtures me.

Whether I'm holding on or letting go—let love guide me, not fear. Amen.

Action Steps: Communication Reset

1. Choose One Relationship to Improve

- It could be a partner, parent, friend, child, or even yourself.

2. Use "I need…" Language

- Practice honest, non-defensive communication.

Examples:

"I need help with dinner when I'm in pain."

"I need emotional support without advice right now."

"I need rest and space when I feel overwhelmed."

3. Set One Small Boundary

This could look like:

- Turning off your phone after 8 PM
- Skipping events that deplete you
- Asking not to talk about your illness unless you bring it up

4. Celebrate Emotional Maturity

- Growth isn't always loud. Sometimes, it's the quiet decision to protect your peace.
- Write down one relationship win this week—even a small one.

Gentle Reminder:

Relationships can evolve. So can you.

You are allowed to change what you need—and still be loved.

You are allowed to choose healing, even if it disappoints others.

Let every boundary be a declaration:

"I am worthy of love, rest, and respect."

Part VIII: Intimacy, Fertility & Sexual Health

Chapter 34: Family Planning with Sickle Cell

Sickle cell anemia is a genetic blood disorder that directly affects family planning. Because of its hereditary nature, couples often face unique and sometimes difficult choices.

Carrier screening, genetic counseling, preimplantation testing, prenatal options, and even adoption are all on the table. None of these decisions are easy, and each couple must weigh risks, values, and faith as they consider the future.

Family planning with sickle cell isn't just about biology—it's about informed decision-making, courage, and love.

Here's how sickle cell anemia plays a role in family planning:

1. Carrier Screening:

- Before having children, individuals can undergo genetic screening to determine if they carry the sickle cell trait (a carrier state, not having the disease but capable of passing the gene on to offspring).
- If both partners are carriers of the sickle cell trait, there's a 25% chance with each pregnancy that their child could inherit two sickle cell genes (one from each parent) and develop sickle cell disease.

2. Genetic Counseling:

- Couples with a family history of sickle cell anemia or who are carriers of the trait may choose to see a genetic counselor. The counselor can provide information about the risks, testing options, and possible outcomes for their children.

3. Preimplantation Genetic Testing (PGT):
- In cases where both parents are carriers of the sickle cell trait, they may opt for in vitro fertilization (IVF) with preimplantation genetic testing to screen embryos for sickle cell disease before implantation. This allows the couple to choose embryos that do not carry the disease.

4. Prenatal Testing:
- If pregnancy occurs and there is a concern about sickle cell, prenatal testing (such as chorionic villus sampling or amniocentesis) can be performed to determine if the fetus has inherited sickle cell disease or the sickle cell trait.

5. Reproductive Decisions:
- Some couples may decide to use assisted reproductive technologies (ART), such as egg or sperm donation, from a non-carrier to avoid the risk of having a child with sickle cell disease.
- Other options include adoption or choosing not to have biological children if the risk of passing on the disease is deemed too high.

6. Informed Decision-Making:
- Family planning decisions are deeply personal and depend on a couple's values, beliefs, and medical advice. Some may choose to have children despite the risk, while others may decide on alternative family-building methods based on the information they have.

Understanding the potential for sickle cell disease in offspring helps families make informed decisions and explore available medical options.

🦋 Pause & Reflect

Family Planning with Sickle Cell

What does family, legacy, and future mean to you in light of sickle cell?

Write down what feels most important to you when considering children and how your health plays a role in those dreams.

Chapter 35: Menstrual Health and Sickle Cell

Menstruation is already a draining monthly reality for many women, but when combined with sickle cell anemia, it can be overwhelming. Hormonal changes, blood loss, dehydration, and pain crises often collide at the same time. This added fatigue increased my risk of experiencing a sickle cell crisis and landing in the hospital.

When I started using an intrauterine device (IUD), one of the benefits was lighter menstrual bleeding—or sometimes no bleeding at all. This turned out to be a game changer. Not only did it help reduce my monthly blood loss, but it also helped me conserve my existing blood levels, which is crucial when you're already living with anemia.

Every woman's body is different, but understanding the connection between menstrual health and sickle cell can empower you to seek solutions instead of suffering in silence.

It's important to consult your physician before starting or changing any medication, including birth control. What worked for me may not work for everyone—but it's worth exploring your options with a trusted healthcare provider.

How menstruation may affect women

1. Increased Risk of Pain Crises

Many people with sickle cell anemia experience pain crises (episodes of intense pain due to blocked blood flow), which can be triggered by various factors, including stress, dehydration, or hormonal changes. Menstrual cycles can increase the frequency and severity of these pain episodes due to the fluctuations in hormones like estrogen and progesterone, which can affect blood flow and increase the risk of vaso-occlusion (when sickled cells block blood vessels).

2. Anemia and Blood Loss

Menstrual bleeding can lead to further blood loss, which may worsen existing anemia in individuals with sickle cell. Since people with sickle cell anemia often already have a lower-than-normal red blood cell count, heavy or prolonged periods could contribute to a drop in hemoglobin levels, leading to symptoms of fatigue, weakness, or dizziness.

3. Hormonal Changes

Hormonal fluctuations during menstruation can exacerbate symptoms like pain or fatigue. For instance, the drop in estrogen levels during menstruation can lead to inflammation, which may increase the intensity of pain crises for someone with sickle cell.

4. Increased Fatigue

The combination of blood loss from menstruation, the added burden on the body from sickle cell anemia, and pain from potential crises can lead to greater levels of fatigue during menstruation. This can make it harder for individuals to manage daily activities or maintain their usual energy levels.

5. Worsened Menstrual Symptoms

People with sickle cell may also experience more severe menstrual symptoms, like cramps (dysmenorrhea), due to the added stress on the body from sickle cell-related complications. The pain and discomfort from menstrual cramps could potentially overlap or be exacerbated by pain crises associated with sickle cell.

6. Impact on Treatment

Menstruation can sometimes complicate treatment for sickle cell anemia. For example, pain medication or treatments (like blood transfusions or iron supplementation) may need to be adjusted during menstruation, depending on the severity of symptoms and blood loss. It's important for those with sickle cell anemia to work with their healthcare provider to manage both sickle cell and menstrual health.

7. Hydration and Blood Flow Issues

Hydration is particularly important for people with sickle cell anemia to prevent sickling of red blood cells. Menstruation can lead to dehydration (especially if there's significant bleeding), which can increase the likelihood of a pain crisis or other complications.

How to Manage:

- Regular Monitoring: Keeping track of menstrual cycles, symptoms, and pain episodes is essential. This helps doctors make informed decisions about pain management and anemia treatment.
- Pain Management: Over-the-counter pain relievers like ibuprofen or acetaminophen may help, but stronger pain management might be necessary for more severe crises.
- Hydration and Nutrition: Staying well-hydrated and eating iron-rich foods during menstruation can help mitigate some of the effects of blood loss and prevent dehydration.

Menstruation can exacerbate some of the challenges faced by individuals with sickle cell anemia, but with proper management, these effects can often be mitigated. It's important for individuals with sickle cell anemia to work closely with their healthcare team to develop a comprehensive plan that addresses both menstrual health and sickle cell-related symptoms.

Talking to Partners About Sickle Cell

Having open conversations with your partner about your health is a form of intimacy and protection.

Conversation Starters:

- "There's something important about my health I'd like you to know…"
- "This condition affects me in ways you might not see, but I want to let you in."
- "Here's how you can support me when I'm in pain…"

Topics to cover:

- Triggers and symptoms
- Fertility concerns or pregnancy risks
- Safe intimacy during crises or low-energy days
- Family planning and genetic testing if considering children

Honesty sets the stage for trust, compassion, and informed choices.

🦋 Reflection | Affirmation | Prayer | Action
Menstrual Health and Sickle Cell

Reflection

How does your menstrual cycle affect your sickle cell symptoms? What patterns have you noticed?

Affirmation

My body is complex, but I am learning to honor and care for it with wisdom and compassion.

Prayer

Lord, give me wisdom to steward my health and courage to seek solutions that ease my suffering. Amen.

Action

Track your next cycle alongside your sickle cell symptoms. Share your notes with your doctor to explore possible management strategies.

Chapter 36: Pregnancy and Sickle Cell

Pregnancy is a sacred gift—and with sickle cell, it is also a risk. I know this firsthand through near-death experiences during childbirth. Carrying life while fighting for your own teaches you that not everyone deserves access to your womb.

Your body, your life, and your children's futures matter. Choosing motherhood with sickle cell requires prayer, preparation, and a supportive medical team.

🦋 Pause & Reflect
Pregnancy and Sickle Cell

What does "sacred" mean to you when you think about pregnancy, your womb, or your ability to nurture life?

Take a moment to write or pray about how you view your body and its boundaries.

Chapter 37: My Pregnancy Journeys with SCD

I became a mother young—with my first daughter, Aoki—my early pregnancy felt smoother, partly because I didn't fully grasp the risks. As life pressures grew, so did the complications. I faced crises, emergency surgeries, ventilators, and even life-and-death decisions for both me and my sister.

Through it all, God carried us. Each child's birth was different, but each reminded me of the fragility and strength of life. Advocacy, preparation, and faith became the anchors that kept us through impossible moments.

Aoki

I had my first child, Aoki, at just 19 years old. I was high risk and low income, so I was offered a lot of free services while pregnant. One of the services I received provided in home nurse car. A nurse would come out and talk to me about my health and how to care for a baby. I learned a lot and asked a lot of questions I was nervous about being a mommy and wanted to learn as much as I could. The pregnancy itself went well I didn't have a crisis and went into labor naturally with my water breaking at home.

I was determined to have a natural birth—and I definitely got one. By the time I asked for pain relief, it was already too late; she was making her way into the world. During the pregnancy, I developed preeclampsia and hypertension, which led to a few extra days in the hospital. Still, we were able to go home together shortly after.

Back then, my stress and worry levels were much lower. They didn't weigh heavily on my pregnancy experience, which in hindsight was a blessing. Despite the pain and complications, everything seemed to go smoothly—probably because I didn't fully understand what could go wrong. I was young, relatively healthy, and admittedly unaware of the seriousness of my condition. But even in that uncertainty, I was incredibly fortunate to bring home a healthy and happy, beautiful baby girl.

Aoki does have a trait and although she does not suffer from sickle cell anemia. She does suffer from anemia. Jen e the ice eating low iron and the constant being cold. So, at around 3 years of age, she suffered a severe drop in her blood levels and a blood transfusion one of the scariest days of my life. But y'all should have saw how cute she was running up and down the halls in her hospital gown and Afro puff.

Layla

My second pregnancy was much more difficult. I believe due to relationship, work and financial stress. I found out I wasn't getting my planned paid maternity leave due to a time delay technicality. So, I was working more picking up shifts to cover the new baby needs and still have enough to cover rent while I was home. But at around 35 weeks pregnant with Layla, I went into a full-blown crisis. Which the doctors were scared would leading me into labor or distress for me and the baby. I of course wanted the same experience of natural labor. But things weren't going as planned. Make matters worse, I was a horrible patient. I fought everybody about everything really, refusing blood transfusions and medications. After days in the hospital, I finally gave into doctors' orders, but it was too late. Just as the transfusion was about to begin, I was rushed in for an emergency C-section.

During surgery, I suffered severe internal bleeding, followed by pulmonary edema. Still unstable after surgery I was placed on a ventilator. The doctors put me into a medically induced coma for three days. I kept waking up and trying to pull the tubes out, I was completely unaware of my condition. Eventually, they had to handcuff me to the bed for my safety.

When I finally came to, I had no idea where my baby was. They told me I was too sick to see her and offered me photos. I wasn't having it. I needed to see her—my actual baby. After throwing the pictures and ripping out my IVs, I made it clear: I was going to the NICU, one way or another. Eventually, they let me visit her—masked, gowned, and still very sick. I finally saw my baby girl. She was jaundiced so they had her under lights, but she was perfect. My beautiful, healthy, happy little girl. Despite everything we had just gone through, she made it. We made it.

Jayden

Before I share my third pregnancy, I want to tell you about my sister's fight with sickle cell disease and her pregnancy journey with Jayden—where I had to step in as his and her advocate.

<u>Picture this</u>: You're at work and you get a call to come quickly to the hospital. Your sister, who's been a patient for a few days, is now in critical condition. You rush there, inform the nurse at the desk who you're there to see, and are escorted down a hallway into an empty conference room.

When you walk in, you see your mom in the corner, her jacket covering most of her face, crying. You ask her what's wrong, but she doesn't answer—just tears. You ask again and again, heart pounding, confused and scared. Still no answer.

Then someone knocks. The door opens. In walks one doctor, then another, and another. Teams of specialists file in until the room—lined with at least 20 chairs—is full. People are standing against the walls. There were people and teams on the conference phones. Lord has mercy.

I was frozen. I looked at my mom and gasped, "Is she dead?"

One of the doctors replied, "No, no—but she's very critical."

They began listing all her complications. I could barely process it. My mom, overwhelmed and heartbroken, had told them she couldn't make any decisions. So, they called me. Me.

My sister had sickle cell disease, and like the year previous —when her lungs collapsed and she had to be airlifted to the University of Michigan—she was now in an even worse condition. But this time, she was pregnant.

She was dying, and so was the baby. Her body was fighting itself, and the baby's presence only intensified it. Their survival rates were both dangerously low. A decision had to be made: who to save.

And they were asking me. Me. Y'all!

I think I blacked out. But God took over my voice. I was there, but I wasn't. I didn't even have time to cry before I started barking orders. Specialists and surgeons introduced themselves—who they were, why they were there. I listened, then told them exactly what we were going to do.

"We are saving them both."

I didn't care what the hospital's typical protocol was. Where I come from, we save the mother and the baby.

So, here's what I did:

Prep her for an emergency C-section. Yes, she's sedated and, on a ventilator, —but don't touch her until the University of Michigan confirms her admittance and the helicopter is on the roof. Once the baby is delivered, send him straight to the NICU. That hospital has a reputation for giving the best care to infants—even if it meant they might not prioritize the mother.

I wasn't going to let that happen.

After more discussion, warnings, and worst-case scenarios—they told me one could survive, or both could die—I stood my ground. The baby was delivered at 23 weeks, weighing just 1 pound, 3 ounces. He spent nearly five months in the NICU, fighting for every breath.

My sister's condition improved slightly after the baby was removed. But she was still critical. While performing the C-section, the doctors discovered the source of her infection: her uterus. A septic uterus—likely the same infection that contributed to her collapsed lungs the year before. If they hadn't operated, they wouldn't have found it. Another impossible decision had to be made: remove her uterus to save her life.

I made the call.

After surgery, she was transferred back to the hospital that had saved her once before. And by the grace of God, they saved her again. She lived almost two more years before her passing. And her son? Our son is still thriving today.

I share this story to say this: having an advocate can mean the difference between life and death.

It's not just about showing up—it's about knowing your loved one's wishes, their condition, and what they would want when they can't speak for themselves. My sister and I were close. I knew her lifestyle, her beliefs, and her will to live—not just for herself, but for her child. I knew she would have wanted me to fight for both of them. And with how sickle cell disease hits our family—especially during pregnancy—her uterus would have continued to make her sicker.

That decision, as painful as it was, was the best for her.

But I wasn't prepared. No one is ever prepared for this. And yet, the choices still must be made.

So please—don't leave your loved ones guessing. Designate someone to advocate for you. Express your wishes clearly, and put them in writing. Let your medical team know your preferences before you're in crisis. Because if no one is there to speak up for you, decisions will be made—and not always in alignment with what you would have wanted.

Being present for your loved ones isn't always pretty. But it must be a priority.

After months of struggle, my sister and my nephew both survived. He came home with me as my son to be cared for and loved. And although my sister passed away a few years later. I'm still thankful I was there to get both through that experience.

Nia

While pregnant with my last child, Nia, at about 30 weeks pregnant I lost my sister. Because of my high-risk pregnancy, I held my stress together the best I could, for as long as I could. Unfortunately, at roughly 36 weeks, I suffered a painful sickle cell crisis. I had to be physically carried because the pain was so bad. Everyone was worried. Being afraid was an understatement, we just lost my sister and here I was pregnant and in an active crisis.

After a few days in the hospital, my crisis subsided. While still in the hospital, my doctors and I decided an elected/scheduled c-section was the safest option. Going into labor naturally could present complications at home and could risk both my life and my baby's. So, we aimed for a more controlled delivery while I was stable and already under care.

The c-section was scheduled for the following morning, and the experience went much smoother than my previous. I learned the hard way not to wait for proper help and care. And God blessed me with another beautiful healthy baby girl.

Looking back, I now understand why doctors once told my mother it was safer if we didn't have children. The strain that pregnancy puts on a body with sickle cell disease is intense and dangerous. At the time, I didn't fully grasp it. But now I do.

Oil and water

Pregnancy and sickle cell don't mix easily. The risks are real. Preparation, a supportive medical team, and a strong personal support system can make all the difference. It's important to carefully consider your health and your partner's when deciding to have children. Pregnancy can be complicated, and the right partner and preparation are crucial.

Pregnancy and childbirth present unique challenges for individuals with sickle cell disease, as the body undergoes significant changes that can heighten the risk of complications for both mother and baby. But with proper planning, informed care, and unwavering faith—many people with SCD go on to have successful pregnancies and raise thriving, healthy, beautiful children.

Here's how pregnancy and childbirth might affect someone with sickle cell disease:

1. Increased Risk of Pain Crises

During pregnancy, the body undergoes numerous changes, including shifts in hormone levels, increased blood volume, and pressure from the growing uterus. These changes can increase the likelihood of sickle cell crises (episodes of severe pain) due to decreased blood flow and oxygen delivery to tissues, especially in the third trimester. Pain crises may be triggered by dehydration, infection, or stress, all of which can be more common during pregnancy.

2. Risk of Complications Related to Anemia

Sickle cell disease causes anemia (a shortage of healthy red blood cells), and pregnancy itself can exacerbate this. Blood volume increases during pregnancy to support the growing fetus, which may strain an already fragile red blood cell supply. In addition, the body's iron needs increase during pregnancy, and if anemia is not properly managed, it can lead to increased fatigue, weakness, and difficulty coping with the demands of pregnancy.

3. Risk of Preeclampsia and Pregnancy-Induced Hypertension

Individuals with sickle cell disease are at higher risk for developing preeclampsia, a serious pregnancy complication characterized by high blood pressure and organ damage. This is particularly concerning because preeclampsia can lead to premature birth, fetal growth restriction, and other complications. The underlying vascular problems in sickle cell disease can make managing blood pressure and other aspects of preeclampsia more challenging.

4. Risk of Stroke

People with sickle cell disease are already at a higher risk of stroke, and pregnancy can increase this risk due to changes in blood pressure, blood flow, and clotting factors. Additionally, dehydration (a common issue during pregnancy) can increase the likelihood of stroke in those with sickle cell disease. Close monitoring of blood pressure and hydration levels is crucial.

5. Risk of Infection

Pregnancy can weaken the immune system, and individuals with sickle cell disease are already more vulnerable to infections, particularly respiratory and urinary tract infections. Infections can trigger pain crises, or they may directly affect the health of the pregnancy. Women with sickle cell disease should be extra vigilant about infection prevention and seek immediate medical attention if any symptoms arise.

6. Premature Birth and Low Birth Weight

Pregnant individuals with sickle cell disease are at an increased risk of preterm labor and delivering a baby with low birth weight. These risks may be related to the reduced blood flow to the placenta, which can affect fetal growth and development. Regular monitoring of fetal health and growth is essential.

7. Blood Clots (Deep Vein Thrombosis)

The increased blood clotting tendency during pregnancy, combined with the vascular issues in sickle cell disease, can increase the risk of deep vein thrombosis (DVT) or pulmonary embolism (PE). These are serious conditions that require careful management to prevent complications.

8. Cesarean Section (C-Section)

Due to the increased risk of complications such as fetal distress, preeclampsia, or other issues, individuals with sickle cell disease may be more likely to require a cesarean section during childbirth. A C-section may also be needed if the baby is in a breech position or if there are other complications during labor.

9. Postpartum Complications

After childbirth, women with sickle cell disease may face complications such as excessive bleeding, delayed wound healing, or an increased risk of infection. The physical demands of childbirth, combined with the stress on the body from sickle cell disease, may delay recovery.

Managing Pregnancy with Sickle Cell Disease:

1. Prenatal Care:

Regular prenatal visits are essential for monitoring both maternal and fetal health. An interdisciplinary healthcare team "including a hematologist, obstetrician, and other specialists" can help manage the risks associated with sickle cell disease during pregnancy.

2. Hydration and Nutrition:

Staying hydrated and maintaining a nutritious diet is especially important during pregnancy to help prevent sickle cell crises and ensure proper fetal development. Iron supplements or other medications may be recommended to manage anemia.

3. Pain Management:

Effective pain management strategies should be developed in advance with healthcare providers to avoid complications during pain crises.

4. Blood Transfusions:

In some cases, blood transfusions may be required during pregnancy to improve oxygen delivery to tissues and reduce the risk of complications. These may help to prevent severe anemia or prevent stroke.

5. Close Monitoring for Complications:

Regular monitoring of blood pressure, fetal growth, and the presence of any signs of preeclampsia or other complications is essential. Blood tests to monitor hemoglobin levels, kidney function, and the overall health of the mother are also important.

6. Emergency Preparedness:

People with sickle cell disease should have a clear plan in place for managing any emergencies, including pain crises or complications, and should be aware of the signs of serious problems like stroke, preeclampsia, or infection.

Pregnancy and childbirth in individuals with sickle cell disease require careful planning and coordination with healthcare providers to minimize risks.

While there are increased risks, many women with sickle cell disease have successful pregnancies with appropriate management.

Close monitoring, pain management, proper hydration, and nutrition are essential for both the mother's and the baby's health throughout the pregnancy and delivery process.

Reflection | Affirmation | Prayer | Action
My Pregnancy Journeys with SCD

Reflection

What moments in your own story (or family's story) remind you of both fragility and resilience?

Affirmation

I am both vulnerable and strong. God's hand sustains me in every season.

Prayer

Lord, thank You for life—for my own and for those I love. Teach me to honor both the risks and the miracles of my journey. Amen.

Action

Share your health wishes and care plan with a trusted advocate. Don't leave life-and-death decisions in the dark.

Chapter 38: Birth Control and Sickle Cell

Birth control isn't one-size-fits-all—especially with sickle cell. Options must be weighed not just for effectiveness, but for how they interact with your body's risks: clotting, anemia, or pain.

Hormonal IUDs, implants, and progestin-only methods may offer safer alternatives than estrogen-based options, while non-hormonal choices carry their own considerations. The key is informed, personalized care.

Types of Birth Control and Considerations for Sickle Cell Anemia:

1. Oral Contraceptives (Pills):

Considerations: Birth control pills that contain estrogen may increase the risk of blood clots, which is a concern for individuals with sickle cell anemia, who may already be at higher risk for clotting and other vascular issues. Progestin-only pills might be a safer option, but they may not be as effective in some cases.

Recommendation: Progestin-only pills or non-oral methods may be preferable to estrogen-containing options.

2. Injectable Contraceptives (Depo-Provera):

Considerations: Depo-Provera is a progestin-only method, which may be a better choice for people with sickle cell anemia since it doesn't contain estrogen. However, it can lead to weight gain, irregular bleeding, and other side effects that need to be managed.

Recommendation: It can be a good option for many individuals but should be monitored carefully by a healthcare provider.

3. IUDs (Intrauterine Devices):

Considerations: Hormonal IUDs release progestin, which makes them a safer option compared to estrogen-containing methods. Non-hormonal IUDs (like the copper IUD) do not have hormones but can cause heavier menstrual bleeding, which might pose a concern for someone with sickle cell anemia, who may already have a higher risk of anemia.

Recommendation: A hormonal IUD may be a suitable choice, but non-hormonal IUDs should be used cautiously.

4. Contraceptive Implants:

Considerations: Similar to IUDs, implants release progestin and are generally considered safe for individuals with sickle cell anemia. They are effective for long-term contraception and do not involve estrogen.

Recommendation: This is often a good choice, offering convenience and effectiveness.

5. Barrier Methods (Condoms, Diaphragms):

Considerations: These methods have no hormonal side effects and are generally safe for individuals with sickle cell anemia. However, they are less effective than other methods and must be used consistently.

Recommendation: Suitable for short-term contraception or when combined with other methods, but not as effective alone.

6. Sterilization:

Considerations: Permanent methods like tubal ligation are an option for individuals who do not want children in the future. This is a non-hormonal option with no risk of side effects related to hormonal contraception.

Recommendation: Considered when the individual is certain they no longer want children.

General Recommendations:

Consult with a healthcare provider: It's crucial to discuss your specific health status and risk factors with a doctor or a gynecologist who understands sickle cell anemia. The choice of birth control should be based on individual health needs and potential risks, such as the likelihood of clotting or complications related to sickle cell disease.

Monitor for complications: Sickle cell disease can sometimes complicate certain medical conditions, so regular follow-up care is essential, particularly with hormonal contraceptive methods.

Pause & Reflect

Birth Control and Sickle Cell

What does "control" mean to you when it comes to your reproductive health?

Write down one question you want to ask your doctor at your next appointment.

Chapter 39: Health Benefits of Birth Control

Beyond pregnancy prevention, birth control—especially hormonal IUDs—can lighten or stop periods, reduce anemia risks, and ease cycle-related crises.

For women with sickle cell, this can be life-changing.

But every option has trade-offs. The goal is not just contraception—it's quality of life.

Below are some potential benefits and considerations of IUDs for Women with Sickle Cell Anemia:

1. Non-Hormonal Options (Copper IUD):

- No hormones involved: A copper IUD does not release hormones, which can be an advantage for women who want to avoid the risks associated with hormonal birth control, such as blood clotting. This is particularly important for women with sickle cell anemia, who may have an increased risk of blood clots.

- Long-term effectiveness: The copper IUD is highly effective (over 99%) and can be used for up to 10 years, providing long-term contraception without needing daily attention or frequent visits to a healthcare provider.

2. Hormonal IUD (e.g., Mirena):

- Progestin-only: Hormonal IUDs release small amounts of progestin, a hormone that thickens cervical mucus and thins the uterine lining. Since it doesn't contain estrogen, the hormonal IUD poses a lower risk of blood clots compared to estrogen-containing methods (like birth control pills or the patch), which is important for someone with sickle cell anemia.

- Reduces heavy periods: A hormonal IUD can significantly reduce or even stop menstruation, which may be beneficial for women with sickle cell anemia who are prone to anemia due to heavy bleeding during periods.

- Reduced menstrual-related pain: Since the hormonal IUD can reduce bleeding and cramping, it may help alleviate symptoms associated with sickle cell, such as painful crises that could be triggered by the physical stress of menstruation.

3. Convenience and Low Maintenance:

- Long-term use with minimal attention: Once inserted, an IUD provides long-term contraception without the need for daily or regular action (such as remembering to take a pill). This can be a convenience factor for women who need to focus on managing sickle cell anemia.

4. Reversible:

- Fertility returns quickly after removal: If a woman decides to become pregnant in the future, fertility typically returns quickly after an IUD is removed. This is important for someone with sickle cell anemia who might want to have children later.

Considerations:

1. Copper IUD and Heavier Periods:

- Heavy bleeding: The copper IUD can increase menstrual bleeding, which may be a concern for someone with sickle cell anemia who is already at risk for anemia or heavy periods. If a woman has a history of significant blood loss due to menstruation, this could worsen anemia and other complications.

- Recommendation: For women with sickle cell anemia who are prone to heavy periods, the hormonal IUD (like Mirena) might be a better option since it helps reduce menstrual flow.

2. Pain and Cramping:

- Initial discomfort: Some women may experience cramps or discomfort when the IUD is first inserted, though this usually improves after a few days to weeks. For women with sickle cell disease, it's important to consider how pain or discomfort could potentially interact with a pain crisis.
- Recommendation: It's important to have the IUD inserted during a time when sickle cell symptoms are well-controlled to minimize the risk of triggering a painful episode.

3. Risk of Infection:

- Infection risk: There is a small risk of infection with IUDs, particularly immediately after insertion. If a woman has compromised immune function or is at higher risk for infections (common in sickle cell patients), this is something to consider.
- Recommendation: Make sure to have a healthcare provider monitor for any signs of infection following IUD insertion.

For women with sickle cell anemia, an IUD "particularly a hormonal one" can be a safe and effective form of birth control, with potential benefits like reduced menstrual bleeding and the avoidance of estrogen-related side effects.

However, it's important to carefully consider the copper IUDs potential to increase menstrual flow and weigh the risk of anemia or heavy bleeding.

Consulting with a healthcare provider who understands sickle cell disease is essential for choosing the best contraceptive method.

They can help monitor potential complications and ensure that the chosen method aligns with the individual's health needs.

🐘 Reflection| Affirmation | Prayer | Action
Health Benefits of Birth Control

Reflection
How does your current birth control (or lack of it) affect your overall health and energy?

Affirmation
I deserve safe, effective options that support both my health and my peace.

Prayer
God, guide me toward wise decisions for my body. May every choice reflect both care for myself and hope for my future. Amen.

Action
If you've been struggling with cycles or pain, schedule a consultation with a provider who understands sickle cell and women's health.

Chapter 40: Understanding Male Health in SCD

Sickle cell affects men and boys uniquely. Delayed puberty, fertility concerns, priapism, emotional isolation, and social pressures are just a few of the struggles often hidden behind silence.

Advocating for their care, normalizing conversations, and creating safe spaces for boys and men to express themselves can transform their journey. They may experience symptoms or emotions they don't fully understand. feeling unheard or overlooked.

By talking with them and helping them better understand their condition, we can empower them to seek help when needed. Teaching them to recognize what's happening in their bodies during episodes of pain can make a big difference.

Helping boys and men cope with their chronic illness using consistent strategies not only supports their current well-being but can also prepare them for adulthood. Representation and mentorship also matter—they need to see thriving men who live with sickle cell too.

Here's how sickle cell anemia can uniquely affect boys and men:

1. **Delayed Growth and Puberty:**
   Boys with sickle cell disease may experience delayed growth and puberty due to the body's struggle to maintain oxygen and energy levels. Their peers might develop faster, which can impact self-esteem and

confidence. It's important to reassure them that these delays are common and often temporary, and to work with a medical team to monitor development.

2. **Testicular Health and Fertility Concerns:**
   In some cases, sickle cell can impact male reproductive health. Repeated sickling episodes can reduce blood flow to organs, including the testicles, potentially affecting sperm production later in life. Some medications, like hydroxyurea, may also affect fertility. It's crucial to have open conversations with healthcare providers about fertility preservation options, especially as boys grow into young men.

3. **Higher Risk of Priapism:**
   Boys and men with sickle cell may suffer from a painful condition called priapism—an unwanted, prolonged erection caused by trapped blood in the penis. If untreated, it can cause permanent damage. This condition can be embarrassing to talk about, especially for adolescents. Creating a safe space for open, nonjudgmental conversation can help them understand it's a medical issue and encourage them to seek immediate care when it happens.

4. **Mental Health and Emotional Resilience:**
   Society often places pressure on boys and men to "tough it out" or suppress their pain. This can lead to emotional isolation, anxiety, and depression. They might not feel comfortable expressing how much they're struggling physically or emotionally. Encourage emotional expression, counseling, and support groups where they can connect with others who understand their journey.

5. **Academic and Social Pressures:**
   Chronic pain episodes and hospital stays can interrupt school and social life, making boys feel left behind or

excluded. Some may feel embarrassed about needing accommodations or special care. Parents, teachers, and caregivers should work as a team to provide academic support and foster a sense of inclusion.

6. **Role Models and Representation:**
Boys and men with chronic illness benefit from seeing others like them thriving. Finding mentors, public figures, or community leaders who live with sickle cell and share their experiences can offer hope and guidance. Representation matters—it reminds them they're not alone and that their lives can be full and meaningful.

More on how sickle cell affects boys and men:

1. Pain Episodes (Crises)

- Sickle cell anemia causes red blood cells to become rigid and shaped like a crescent moon (sickle-shaped), which can block blood flow, leading to pain episodes called sickle cell crises. These crises are the hallmark of the disease and can occur at any time, but are often triggered by dehydration, infections, or extreme temperatures.

- In boys, the pain episodes typically begin in early childhood and may continue throughout life. The pain can occur in various parts of the body, including the chest, back, arms, legs, and abdomen.

- For men, these pain crises can persist into adulthood and affect their ability to perform daily tasks, engage in work, or participate in physical activities.

2. Fatigue and Low Energy

- Sickle cell anemia leads to a shortage of healthy red blood cells (anemia), which means less oxygen is carried throughout the body. This can cause extreme fatigue and weakness, which affects daily life and productivity.

- Boys with sickle cell anemia may experience delayed physical development due to constant fatigue, while adult men may have challenges with work, social activities, or physical tasks due to low energy levels.

3. Risk of Stroke

- Sickle cell anemia increases the risk of stroke, particularly in young children. The abnormal sickle-shaped cells can block blood vessels in the brain, leading to a stroke.
- This risk remains throughout life, but men with sickle cell disease tend to have a higher risk of stroke compared to women.

4. Organ Damage

- Over time, sickle cell anemia can cause damage to organs due to blocked blood flow and oxygen deprivation. Kidneys, liver, and lungs can be affected, leading to chronic health problems such as kidney failure, lung disease, and liver damage.
- In men, sickle cell anemia can also cause complications related to sexual health, including erectile dysfunction, especially in older age, due to poor blood flow.

5. Increased Risk of Infection

- Sickle cell anemia can impair the immune system, making it harder for the body to fight infections. This is especially true for children, but men can also experience frequent infections, particularly related to the lungs (pneumonia) or bones (osteomyelitis).

- Infections can sometimes trigger a sickle cell crisis, leading to more severe pain and other complications.

6. Bone and Joint Problems

- Over time, sickle cell anemia can cause bone damage and lead to joint pain, especially in the hips, shoulders, and knees. This is a result of poor blood flow to the bones and joints, causing damage and inflammation.
- For boys, this can result in difficulties with physical activities and growth. In men, it may cause chronic pain and disability.

7. Mental Health Impact

- Chronic pain, frequent hospital visits, and the physical limitations caused by sickle cell anemia can affect the mental health of boys and men.
- Anxiety, depression, and stress are common among individuals living with sickle cell anemia due to the constant management of the condition and the limitations it imposes on their lives.
- Boys may experience emotional and psychological effects as they struggle with the challenges of growing up with a chronic illness, while adult men may face increased stress as they juggle family, work, and health issues.

8. Life Expectancy

- While life expectancy for people with sickle cell anemia has improved with medical advancements, the disease still impacts longevity. Men with sickle cell anemia may face a shorter life expectancy due to complications such as organ damage, stroke, and infections.

9. Sexual and Reproductive Health

- Sickle cell anemia can affect sexual health in men, leading to issues such as erectile dysfunction or reduced fertility, often due to poor blood flow and damage to reproductive organs.

- While men with sickle cell anemia can father children, they may experience difficulties related to the complications of the disease.

Sickle cell anemia affects boys and men through a combination of painful episodes, fatigue, organ damage, and potential mental health challenges.

While boys may experience growth and developmental issues, men face the long-term effects of chronic pain, reduced organ function, and other complications.

Managing sickle cell anemia often requires ongoing medical care, lifestyle adjustments, and psychological support to help cope with the physical and emotional toll the disease can take.

🦋 Pause & Reflect

Understanding Male Health in SCD

Think of a boy or man in your life who may be carrying silent struggles.

How can you check in, encourage, or advocate for him this week?

Part VIII: Intimacy, Fertility & Sexual Health
Reflection | Affirmation | Prayer | Action

Worthy of Love—Body, Soul, and Story

A guided pause to reclaim your relationship with your body, intimacy, and emotional connection.

Reflection: Intimacy, Image, and Identity

Your body is not broken—it is brave.

Your story is not too much—it is sacred.

1. What have you believed (or been told) about your body since your diagnosis or pregnancy?
2. What do you grieve about your physical changes—and what do you want to celebrate?
3. How do you want to feel in your body?

Write down 3 words you want to embody:

Examples: safe, soft, empowered, wanted, radiant, cherished, confident.

Affirmation: My Body Is Still Worthy of Love

"I am more than my symptoms.

I am not defined by pain or fatigue.

My body is not perfect—but it is powerful.

I deserve tenderness, connection, and love in every season.

I am still worthy. I am still whole."

Prayer: Help Me See My Body with Loving Eyes

Dear God,

Some days, my body feels like it betrays me. But You see it as beautiful—still strong, still sacred. Help me release shame and reclaim softness.

Help me speak kindly to myself and invite intimacy with honesty and grace. Bless my relationships with trust, communication, and care.

When I don't feel desirable, remind me I am deeply loved—not just for what I do, but for who I am.

Give me the confidence to embrace connection and the courage to speak my needs. Amen.

Action Steps: Restoring Intimacy with Yourself and Others

1. Create One Ritual of Self-Connection

This could be:

- Touching your skin with care (lotion, massage, gentle stretch)
- Wearing something that makes you feel good
- Looking at yourself in the mirror and speaking love over your body

2. Start One Honest Conversation with Your Partner (or Yourself)

Use prompts like:

- "Sometimes I feel distant because of pain. Here's what helps me reconnect…"

- "What makes you feel emotionally close to me?"
- "Can we create moments of intimacy that honor where I am right now?"

3. Redefine What Intimacy Looks Like

List 3 non-sexual ways you feel close to someone:

- Cuddling or sitting in silence
- Eye contact or affirming words
- Laughing together or reminiscing

Schedule a "closeness moment" that's pressure-free and joy-filled.

Gentle Reminder:

Intimacy is not only about the physical—it's about presence, trust, and emotional safety.

You are allowed to show up as you are, ask for what you need, and love your body through every phase.

Your softness is strength.

Your truth is intimacy.

Your body is not a burden—it's a vessel of love.

Part IX: Mastering the Healthcare Maze

Chapter 41: Navigating Healthcare Systems

Navigating healthcare systems is one of the most challenging parts of living with sickle cell disease (SCD). It involves managing complex care needs, understanding your rights, and learning how to advocate for yourself or a loved one.

From building strong relationships with doctors, understanding insurance, and preparing for emergencies, to exploring clinical trials and legal protections, the healthcare maze can feel overwhelming. But with preparation and advocacy, you can create a path that supports both your health and your peace of mind.

Tips to help navigate healthcare systems effectively:

1. Building a Strong Relationship with Healthcare Providers

Choose the Right Medical Team: Sickle cell disease often requires a multidisciplinary approach. Your medical team may include:

- Primary Care Physician (PCP): To manage overall health and coordinate care.

- Hematologist: A specialist in blood disorders, critical for managing sickle cell disease.

- Pain Management Specialists: To help manage chronic pain and prevent crises.

- Pediatricians (for children with sickle cell): They provide care tailored to kids and guide parents.

- Other Specialists: Depending on complications, you may need nephrologists (kidneys), cardiologists (heart), pulmonologists (lungs), orthopedists (bones), and other specialists.

- Establish Open Communication: Build a relationship with your doctors based on trust. Be honest about your symptoms, concerns, and the challenges you're facing. This open dialogue helps them provide better, personalized care.

- Regular Check-Ups: Regular visits are crucial to monitor disease progression, address issues like organ damage, and prevent or manage crises.

2. Advocating for Yourself or a Loved One

- Know Your Rights: Understand your rights, especially in terms of healthcare access and treatment. In many countries, there are laws in place to protect patients from discrimination due to illness or disability.

- Be Your Own Advocate: If you feel that your concerns aren't being heard, don't be afraid to ask questions or seek second opinions. Keep track of symptoms, treatments, and side effects so you can provide specific information during appointments.

- Bring a Support Person: It's often helpful to bring a family member, friend, or caregiver to medical appointments. They can help take notes, ask questions, and provide emotional support.

- Prepare for Appointments: Write down your symptoms, questions, and any changes in your condition before your visit. This ensures that you don't forget anything important during the consultation.

3. Understanding Your Insurance and Healthcare Costs

- Know Your Coverage: Health insurance policies can vary widely, so it's important to fully understand what your insurance plan covers. Sickle cell treatments, hospitalizations, medications, and specialist visits can be expensive, and knowing your coverage can help you avoid unexpected costs.

- Check Coverage for Specific Treatments: Some insurance plans may limit coverage for certain treatments or medications (like hydroxyurea or blood transfusions). Verify which medications and therapies are covered under your plan.

- Understand Out-of-Pocket Costs: Be aware of co-pays, deductibles, and out-of-pocket maximums. Understanding these costs ahead of time can help you plan financially, especially if you're expecting to undergo a treatment or hospitalization.

- Financial Assistance Programs: If your insurance doesn't cover the full cost of treatment or if you are uninsured, inquire about financial assistance programs. Many hospitals and clinics have funds available to help low-income patients with sickle cell disease. Additionally, drug manufacturers sometimes offer patient assistance programs for expensive medications.

4. Seeking Specialists and Accessing Specialized Care

- Referral Process: If you're seeing a primary care physician, they can refer you to specialists like a hematologist. If you're already seeing a specialist, they may help guide you to other providers as needed.

- Find Sickle Cell Centers: There are specialized sickle cell disease centers that offer comprehensive care. These centers focus on managing the specific needs of individuals with sickle cell disease, including regular blood tests, genetic counseling, and access to clinical trials.

- Consider Centers of Excellence: Some hospitals or medical institutions are designated as "Centers of Excellence" for sickle cell care. These institutions have expertise in managing complex cases and often have access to cutting-edge treatments and research.

- Telehealth Options: Telemedicine can be a valuable resource for accessing specialists, especially if you're in a rural area or unable to travel frequently for appointments. Many hematologists and other specialists offer virtual consultations.

5. Managing Emergency Care

- Know When to Seek Emergency Care: Sickle cell pain crises, infections, or complications like acute chest syndrome can require immediate medical attention. It's important to know when your symptoms require an ER visit.

- Communicate Your Condition: When seeking emergency care, make sure to inform the healthcare team that you have sickle cell disease. Carry a medical ID card that indicates your condition. This ensures that the medical staff understands the nature of your illness and provides the most appropriate care.

- Create an Emergency Plan: Work with your healthcare provider to develop an emergency plan that outlines how to manage pain crises or other complications. This plan should include information on what medications to take, who to contact, and how to access immediate care if needed.

6. Managing Pain Crises

- Pain Management Plans: Having a structured pain management plan in place is crucial. Work with your healthcare providers to develop an individualized plan that includes both medical and non-medical approaches (like hydration, rest, heat, and relaxation techniques).

- Document and Report Crises: Keep a record of when pain crises occur, their duration, and their intensity. This information can help doctors identify patterns, triggers, and provide better pain management strategies. Hydration and Prevention: Staying hydrated is key to preventing pain crises, as dehydration can trigger episodes. Discuss with your healthcare provider how much fluid intake is recommended and whether any other preventative measures are necessary.

7. Accessing Clinical Trials and Research Opportunities

- Stay Informed About New Treatments: There are ongoing clinical trials studying new treatments for sickle cell disease, including gene therapy and new medications. Ask your healthcare provider if there are any clinical trials you may be eligible for.

- Advocate for Participation: If you're interested in participating in a clinical trial, ask your doctors about available studies. Clinical trials can sometimes provide access to experimental treatments that aren't yet widely available.

- Understand the Risks and Benefits: Before joining a trial, ensure you fully understand the potential benefits, risks, and what the study will involve. Research coordinators can provide this information.

8. Navigating Healthcare Systems in Different Environments

- International Considerations: If you're seeking care outside your home country, it's important to understand how healthcare systems differ, including how treatments for sickle cell are managed, the availability of medications, and how to navigate healthcare costs. In some countries, sickle cell care may not be as readily accessible.
- Advocacy and Awareness: Depending on where you live, sickle cell disease may not be as well understood. Be prepared to educate healthcare providers and advocate for the treatment you need.

9. Support Resources

- Support Groups: Many organizations provide support groups for people with sickle cell disease. These groups can be a great resource for emotional support, tips on navigating healthcare systems, and sharing personal experiences. Local and online communities can be especially helpful.
- Sickle Cell Organizations: Organizations like the Sickle Cell Disease Association of America (SCDAA) and other national and international groups provide resources, advocacy, and information on navigating healthcare systems. They may also offer guidance on insurance issues, legal protections, and financial assistance.

- Patient Advocacy: If you're struggling with insurance denials, discrimination, or challenges accessing care, there are patient advocacy organizations and legal services that can help fight for your rights.

10. Understanding Legal Protections

- Disability and Employment Rights: In many countries, individuals with sickle cell disease are protected by disability rights laws (like the Americans with Disabilities Act in the U.S.). These laws ensure that you are treated fairly in workplaces and can access accommodations for your condition, including time off for medical appointments or pain crises.

- Educational Rights for Children: If you or a family member with sickle cell is in school, laws may ensure that children with chronic conditions receive the accommodations they need, including extra time for assignments, breaks for hydration, and protection from discrimination.

By taking a proactive and informed approach, you can successfully navigate the healthcare system to manage sickle cell disease.

It's important to advocate for your needs, seek out the appropriate specialists, and make sure that your care is comprehensive.

And don't hesitate to seek support from healthcare professionals, patient advocacy organizations, and peers who understand the challenges of living with sickle cell disease.

🦬 Reflection | Affirmation | Prayer | Action
Navigating Healthcare Systems

Reflection

How confident do you feel right now about navigating your healthcare system? Where do you feel the most stuck?

Affirmation

I am not powerless in my healthcare. I can learn, prepare, and advocate for myself with wisdom and courage.

Prayer

Lord, guide me as I navigate this system. Help me find the right doctors, resources, and support so I can walk in strength and not in fear. Amen.

Action

Write down the names and contact info of your core care team (PCP, hematologist, ER doctor, etc.) and keep it in your phone or wallet.

Chapter 42: Discrimination in Healthcare

Once while working in a hospital coffee shop, I overheard nurses doubting a sickle cell patient's pain, assuming she was only there for medication. It broke my heart because I've lived through those same accusations. Their words reminded me how damaging bias can be—especially when it comes from the very people meant to care for us.

These were people I laughed and joked with regularly—people I genuinely liked. Which made it even more disheartening to hear. They talked about how much of a "hassle" it was to care for someone like me. Of course, they didn't know I had the disease, but still, it stung.

I confided in a close coworker Charlena, who brought it up with them privately. She understood how I felt, she also had a loved one who lives with sickle cell anemia and didn't play about our feelings.

They did later apologize, and I appreciated that. But the experience reminded me that this kind of thing happens far too often.

Discrimination against people with SCD often shows up as disbelief, under-treatment, or stereotyping. These often come from a lack of awareness, misunderstanding, or outright prejudice about the nature of the condition.

What hurts most is that it can delay care and put lives at risk. Compassion and understanding cost nothing, yet they can change everything.

People with SCD may face stigma both in healthcare settings and in their daily lives. This can take a toll on their emotional well-being, limit their access to proper care, and affect their overall quality of life.

Just because you don't fully understand what someone is going through doesn't make their experience any less real.

Here are some challenges related to discrimination and stigma:

1. Misunderstanding of the Disease:

- Invisible Illness: Sickle cell disease is often invisible, meaning that others cannot see when a person is in pain or experiencing a crisis. This can lead to the misconception that the individual is not truly sick or is exaggerating their symptoms. This lack of understanding can lead to skepticism, dismissiveness, or disbelief when someone with sickle cell disease requests accommodations or expresses their need for rest during a pain crisis.

- Stereotyping: Because sickle cell disease is most common in people of African descent (though it also affects other populations), there can be racial and cultural stereotyping. People with sickle cell may be unfairly labeled as "complainers" or "drug-seekers" because of the need for pain management or hospitalization during crises, leading to judgment or a lack of empathy from others, including medical professionals.

2. Discrimination in Healthcare:

- Lack of Understanding from Healthcare Providers: Not all healthcare professionals are adequately trained in sickle cell disease, and this can result in a lack of understanding or even biased treatment. Some patients may face discrimination when seeking pain relief, as medical professionals may mistakenly believe they are exaggerating pain or seeking opioids for non-medical reasons. This can lead to delays in treatment, mistreatment, or reluctance to provide adequate care.

- Inadequate Pain Management: The difficulty in managing pain effectively in sickle cell disease is a common frustration. Patients with sickle cell disease may face discrimination if their pain is not taken seriously by healthcare providers, leading to inadequate pain management during crises or hospitalization.

3. Social Stigma and Isolation:

- Social Rejection: People with sickle cell disease may face discrimination in social settings, including among peers, family members, and colleagues, especially when they need to take breaks, miss events, or avoid physical activities due to their condition. The need for rest during a crisis or the unpredictability of symptoms may cause others to view the individual as unreliable, "weak," or "fragile," leading to social isolation or exclusion.

- Fear of Burdening Others: Many individuals with sickle cell disease feel the pressure of not wanting to burden their loved ones with their condition. This can lead to them hiding their symptoms or minimizing their struggles, even though they may need help. This "hidden suffering" can create emotional distress, as they may feel misunderstood or alienated.

4. Employment and Education Challenges:

- Job Discrimination: People with sickle cell disease may encounter challenges in the workplace. Their chronic illness may lead to absenteeism, periods of illness, or reduced ability to perform at their usual level, which can lead to discrimination from employers. In some cases, they may face issues with not receiving reasonable accommodations, like flexibility for medical appointments or time off during crises.

- Academic Struggles: For students with sickle cell disease, the challenges of frequent absences or physical limitations due to pain or fatigue can make it difficult to keep up with schoolwork. This may result in academic discrimination, lower expectations, or lack of support from teachers or peers.

🐾 Pause & Reflect

Discrimination in Healthcare

Think of a time you felt misunderstood or judged in a healthcare setting.

How did it affect you?

How might you respond differently next time—with self-advocacy, support, or educating others?

Chapter 43: Coping with Discrimination & Stigma

Discrimination and stigma carry emotional, social, and even physical consequences. But by educating others, advocating for yourself, building a strong support network, and caring for your emotional health, you can stand stronger against them.

Openness, self-advocacy, peer support, counseling, and stress management are tools that not only help you cope but also help you thrive.

Stigma often comes from ignorance, but your resilience can break the cycle.

1. Educating Others:

- Raising Awareness: One of the most effective ways to combat stigma is through education. People with sickle cell disease can take the opportunity to educate others about their condition, its challenges, and its impact on daily life. This can help reduce misconceptions and foster understanding, especially among friends, family, and colleagues. It may also be beneficial to share resources such as brochures or websites that provide accurate information about sickle cell disease.

- Being Open About the Disease: Although it can be uncomfortable, being open about sickle cell disease with friends, family, and coworkers can help them better understand the individual's needs and challenges. When people are informed about what sickle cell is and how it affects the body, they are more likely to respond with empathy and support.

2. **Advocacy and Empowerment:**
    - Self-Advocacy: People with sickle cell disease can benefit from learning how to advocate for themselves in healthcare settings, at work, and in social situations. This can involve speaking up about the need for pain management, requesting reasonable accommodations, or educating others when discrimination occurs. Being empowered to ask for what is needed and to set boundaries can help counteract the stigma and discrimination they face.
    - Legal Protections: In many countries, there are legal protections against discrimination based on medical conditions, such as the Americans with Disabilities Act (ADA) in the United States. Individuals with sickle cell disease can familiarize themselves with their rights and seek legal recourse if they face discrimination in the workplace or healthcare setting.

3. **Building a Support Network:**
    - Peer Support: Connecting with other individuals who have sickle cell disease can be a powerful way to combat feelings of isolation and stigma. Support groups, either in-person or online, provide a safe space for individuals to share their experiences, exchange coping strategies, and offer mutual support. These communities can be a source of validation, as members can relate to the challenges each other faces.
    - Family Support: Family members can be advocates and sources of emotional support. By learning more about sickle cell disease, families can help challenge stigma within their communities and ensure that the person with sickle cell is treated with understanding and dignity.

- Mental Health Support: Therapy or counseling can help individuals process feelings of discrimination, stigma, and isolation. Talking to a mental health professional can provide individuals with tools to manage the emotional impact of stigma and help them develop healthy coping strategies.

4. Managing Stress and Emotional Well-being:

- Stress Management: Stress can exacerbate sickle cell symptoms, so it's important to find ways to manage emotional strain. Techniques such as mindfulness, deep breathing, journaling, or engaging in relaxing hobbies can help reduce stress levels and improve emotional well-being. Keeping stress in check can make it easier to navigate the challenges of discrimination and stigma.
- Building Resilience: Many individuals with sickle cell disease develop resilience through their experiences. Learning to accept the things that cannot be changed, focusing on strengths, and staying positive can help people with sickle cell maintain mental and emotional health. Recognizing that it's okay to seek help and to have bad days is crucial to self-compassion and emotional balance.

5. Seeking Professional Help for Emotional Health:

- Therapy or Counseling: Professional help, such as therapy, can be beneficial for those who struggle with the emotional and psychological impact of discrimination. Cognitive behavioral therapy (CBT) can help individuals identify and change negative thought patterns, while support groups for chronic illness can provide community and shared experiences.

- Addressing Depression or Anxiety: Stigma and discrimination can lead to or exacerbate depression, anxiety, and other mental health conditions. It's important to seek appropriate support, including counseling or medications, if necessary, to address mental health needs.

It's important to recognize that stigma often arises from a lack of awareness and understanding, so efforts to educate others about the condition can go a long way in reducing prejudice and fostering compassion.

While it's difficult to overcome all forms of discrimination, empowering individuals with the tools to cope and stand up for their rights can help mitigate the emotional impact and improve their overall quality of life.

Reflection | Affirmation | Prayer | Action
Coping with Discrimination and Stigma

Reflection

How do you usually respond to stigma—by withdrawing, getting angry, or pushing through silently? What healthier response could you try?

Affirmation

I will not be defined by stigma. I am worthy of respect, care, and compassion.

Prayer

God, when I feel judged or unseen, remind me that You see me fully and love me completely. Give me strength to stand tall in the face of bias. Amen.

Action

Share one fact about sickle cell with someone in your circle this week. Education begins one conversation at a time.

Chapter 44: Being a Proactive Patient

For years, I neglected my health—skipped appointments, ignored aftercare plans, and misused medication by not taking it or being inconsistent. It nearly cost me my life. I learned the hard way that playing fast and loose with your health is not worth it.

Being a proactive patient means partnering with your medical team, tracking your health, asking questions, and building support systems. It's about taking ownership of your care—not out of fear, but out of love for your life and your future.

Work with your care team, not against them. That's how you get the care you truly deserve.

Here are some tips:

1. Educate Yourself About Your Condition

- Know your diagnosis: Understand your specific type of sickle cell disease (e.g., sickle cell anemia vs. sickle cell trait) and its symptoms, complications, and treatment options.
- Stay informed: Keep up-to-date with new treatments, research, and advancements related to sickle cell anemia. This will help you feel more confident in conversations with doctors and empower you to make informed decisions about your care.

2. Maintain Open and Honest Communication

- Be clear about your symptoms: When describing your pain or symptoms, be as specific as possible. Explain how you feel, the intensity of your pain, when it started, and anything that may have triggered it. This helps your healthcare team understand your condition better and adjust treatment accordingly.

- Ask questions: Don't be afraid to ask questions if something is unclear. You deserve to understand your treatment options, the side effects of medications, and the potential outcomes.

- Be upfront about your concerns: If you're worried about your treatment plan, side effects, or have doubts, let your healthcare provider know. Transparency helps you and your doctor make better decisions.

3. Track Your Health and Symptoms

- Keep a journal: Track pain episodes, any potential triggers (like stress, dehydration, or temperature changes), medications you've taken, and any other health changes. This will help you spot patterns and make more effective decisions about your care.

- Record key information: Write down vital stats such as your medications, dosages, appointment dates, test results, and any changes in your condition. This information can be very helpful in follow-up appointments.

4. Build a Support System

- Involve family and friends: Share your condition and treatment plan with close family and friends. They can help you manage your care, recognize when you might need help, and advocate for you during medical appointments.

- Connect with support groups: Join support groups for people with sickle cell anemia. These groups offer emotional support, as well as advice on managing the condition and navigating the healthcare system.

5. Be Assertive in Appointments

- Prepare in advance: Write down key points you want to discuss with your doctor ahead of time. This ensures that you don't forget important issues and helps make your appointments more productive.
- Don't accept rushed answers: If a healthcare provider gives you a quick answer that doesn't fully address your concerns, politely ask for further explanation. You have the right to feel heard and understood.

6. Know Your Rights as a Patient

- Understand patient rights: Be aware of your rights within the healthcare system, including the right to seek a second opinion or change doctors if you feel your needs aren't being met.
- Be your own advocate: If you feel that something isn't right, whether it's with your care plan or the way you're being treated, speak up. You can politely request a meeting with a different healthcare provider or a patient advocate at the hospital to discuss your concerns.

7. Set Realistic Expectations and Take Care of Yourself

- Manage your energy: Sickle cell anemia can cause fatigue, so prioritize your health by getting enough rest, staying hydrated, and eating well. Don't push yourself too hard and listen to your body when it tells you to slow down.
- Set achievable goals: Whether it's in managing pain or your daily routine, set goals that are attainable and

give yourself credit for making progress. Be patient with yourself as you navigate your condition.

8. Know When to Seek Emergency Care

- Recognize warning signs: Be aware of when symptoms may require urgent care. For example, if you experience severe pain, difficulty breathing, signs of stroke, or high fever, seek medical attention immediately. Having this knowledge helps you act swiftly and avoid complications.

9. Develop a Plan for Pain Management

- Discuss pain management options: Work with your healthcare team to create an effective pain management plan. This may include medications, physical therapy, relaxation techniques, or alternative therapies. Knowing what works for you can help you advocate for the best approach.

- Be proactive: Don't wait until you're in severe pain to ask for help. If you feel a pain episode coming on, inform your healthcare provider early so they can help you manage it before it worsens.

10. Be Open to Adjusting Your Care Plan

- Collaborate with your doctor: Treatment plans can evolve over time as your condition changes. Regularly reassess your approach with your doctor, especially if your current treatment isn't working as effectively as it used to.

- Don't be afraid to try new treatments: While it's important to make informed decisions, be open to exploring new treatment options, including clinical trials or medications, that could improve your quality of life.

11. Advocate for Sickle Cell Awareness

- Raise awareness: Use your experience to educate others about sickle cell anemia. By sharing your story, you can help reduce stigma, raise awareness, and improve support systems for people with the condition.
- Get involved: Participate in advocacy efforts for sickle cell research, policy changes, or access to better care. Your voice can help shape the future of treatment and support for individuals with sickle cell anemia.

Being an empowered patient and advocate involves staying informed, communicating clearly, tracking your health, and building a support network. Taking a proactive role in your healthcare and knowing when and how to advocate for your needs will help you manage sickle cell anemia more effectively and improve your overall quality of life.

Pause & Reflect

Being a Proactive Patient

Where are you on the patient spectrum right now—passive, reactive, or proactive?

Write down one step you can take this month to move toward being more engaged in your healthcare.

Chapter 45: Hospital Preparedness Guide

Emergencies don't wait. Being prepared for the hospital—whether it's a sudden crisis or a planned procedure—can make all the difference. The more prepared you are, the less you'll need to scramble during a crisis.

From having a go-bag ready to keeping updated medical records, to assigning trusted advocates, hospital preparedness reduces fear and chaos during stressful moments. Preparation is an act of both wisdom and love for yourself and those who may need to care for you.

Here are practical steps to ensure you are well-prepared for these situations:

1. Create an Emergency Plan

Develop a Care Plan with Your Doctor: Work with your healthcare provider to create a detailed emergency care plan. This should include:

- Signs and symptoms that indicate when to seek emergency care (e.g., severe pain, fever, difficulty breathing).

- Step-by-step instructions on what to do if you're experiencing a crisis, including medication dosages, hydration, and any other recommendations.

- Contact information for your healthcare team, including your primary care doctor, hematologist, and pain management specialist.

- Hospital preferences: List which hospitals or emergency rooms have experience with sickle cell disease and can provide the specialized care you need.

2. Maintain a Personal Medical Record

Medical History: Keep an updated record of your medical history, including:

- Your sickle cell diagnosis and any complications you've experienced.
- Medications you're currently taking (dosages and frequency).
- Previous hospitalizations or surgeries related to sickle cell disease.
- Known allergies to medications, foods, or other substances.
- Other health conditions that may impact your treatment (e.g., asthma, diabetes, hypertension).
- Emergency Contact List: Have a list of emergency contacts, including family members, caregivers, or friends who can assist you if needed.
- Document of Advance Directives or DNR (Do Not Resuscitate) instructions, if applicable.

3. Pack an Emergency Kit

Keep a bag or box packed with essentials that you may need during an emergency or hospital stay. This should include:

- Important documents (e.g., identification, insurance information, medical records).
- Medications: A list of all your medications and doses, as well as any emergency medications you take regularly (e.g., painkillers, antibiotics).

- Hydration supplies: Bottled water, electrolyte solutions, or oral rehydration salts to keep you hydrated, especially during a pain crisis.
- Comfort items: Blankets, pillows, or personal items that make hospital stays more comfortable (like books, headphones, or entertainment).
- Medical supplies: If you use a particular device (e.g., nebulizer, CPAP for sleep apnea), make sure it's readily available. Don't forget spare batteries for devices if necessary.
- Snacks and food: Keep a small supply of easily digestible snacks in case you're unable to eat regular meals.
- Emergency contact list: Include a written list of people to contact if you're hospitalized (family members, friends, caregivers).

4. Know When to Go to the Hospital

- Recognize a Pain Crisis: Understand the warning signs of a sickle cell pain crisis, including:
- Sudden, intense pain that doesn't respond to over-the-counter painkillers.
- Pain in areas like the chest, abdomen, or bones that becomes severe and persistent.
- Pain that interferes with normal daily activities.
- Fever or signs of infection, which could indicate a serious complication (e.g., acute chest syndrome or sepsis).
- Other Emergency Situations: Be aware of other emergencies related to sickle cell, including:

- Stroke symptoms (sudden weakness, difficulty speaking, confusion).
- Breathing difficulty (potential acute chest syndrome or lung complications).
- Severe dehydration or exhaustion that doesn't resolve with fluids.
- Seek Immediate Help: If you experience any of the above symptoms or feel that your condition is worsening, go to the hospital or call emergency services right away. Sickle cell disease requires timely intervention to prevent serious complications.

5. Prepare for a Hospital Stay

- Pre-Admission Process: If you know you'll need to be hospitalized for a planned procedure or treatment, try to pre-register with the hospital. This speeds up the admission process.
- Emergency Department (ED): If you're heading to the emergency room (ER) for a crisis, be ready to communicate your condition clearly to the medical team.

You can:

- Carry an ID card: A medical ID card stating that you have sickle cell disease and what treatments you need can help in emergencies.
- Have your care plan handy: Bring the care plan or have it on your phone, if possible. It should detail your treatment preferences (medications, pain management, and fluids).
- Advocate for yourself: If you feel your pain is being underestimated, advocate for yourself or ask a family

member to help communicate the urgency of your condition.

6. Coordinate with Family and Caregivers

- Emergency Contacts: Have a reliable family member, friend, or caregiver who knows your medical history and who can assist with decision-making in case you cannot communicate clearly during an emergency.

- Explain Your Needs: Ensure that the people around you know what to do in an emergency, how to handle your pain management needs, and how to contact your healthcare providers.

- Assign Roles: If possible, assign specific roles to trusted individuals (e.g., one person can gather documents, another can contact the doctor, etc.).

7. Keep Track of Pain Crises

- Pain Journal: Keep a log of your pain levels, triggers, and any changes you experience. This information can help healthcare providers manage your care more effectively, especially if the pain becomes more severe or frequent.

- Document Crisis History: Note the intensity, location, and duration of past pain crises. Share this history with your medical team to guide future treatment and prevent unnecessary delays in care.

8. Prepare for Post-Hospital Care

- Follow-Up Appointments: Make sure to schedule follow-up visits with your hematologist or care team after being discharged from the hospital. These appointments are crucial for monitoring your recovery and managing your sickle cell disease.

- Home Care Instructions: If you need home care after discharge, ensure that all necessary prescriptions, supplies, and instructions are clearly documented. If you have a caregiver, they should be trained on how to assist with your recovery (e.g., medication administration, hydration, wound care).

- Recovery Support: If you have physical or emotional needs after a hospital stay (e.g., rehabilitation, mental health support), reach out to support groups or therapy resources to assist with your recovery.

9. Plan for Hospitalization During Travel

- Travel Preparations: If you're traveling away from home, research nearby hospitals or sickle cell centers in the area. Having this information ahead of time can save valuable time in an emergency.

- Travel Medical Kit: Pack a travel kit with extra medications, documentation, and emergency contact information.

- Alert Your Travel Companions: Let anyone traveling with you know about your condition and emergency protocols.

10. Use Technology for Support

- Emergency Apps: Consider using health management apps that store your medical information, medications, and emergency contacts. Some apps also allow you to send this information to emergency responders if necessary.

- Telehealth Services: Some providers offer virtual consultations. If you're unsure whether you need to go to the ER, you can contact your healthcare provider via telemedicine for guidance.

11. Mental and Emotional Preparation

- Mental Health Support: Hospital stays and emergencies can be stressful, so it's important to take care of your mental health as well. Consider mindfulness techniques, relaxation exercises, or talking to a counselor about your experiences.

- Support Networks: Having support from family, friends, or a support group for people with SCD can help reduce anxiety around hospital stays and emergencies.

By taking these steps, you can better manage emergency situations and hospitalizations, ensuring that you're prepared for any unexpected events related to sickle cell disease.

It also allows you to take a proactive approach in managing your health, giving you peace of mind knowing that you have a clear plan in place.

🦬 Reflection | Affirmation | Prayer | Action Hospital Preparedness Guide

Reflection

If you had to go to the hospital tonight, would you or your family know where everything is? What would you wish you had ready?

Affirmation

I am preparing today so I can face tomorrow with calm and confidence.

Prayer

Lord, help me prepare wisely so that when emergencies come, I can move in peace instead of panic. Amen.

Action

Start your hospital go-bag this week. Add at least three essentials (documents, comfort items, or medication lists).

Chapter 46: Future of Sickle Cell Treatments

The future of SCD care is full of hope. Gene therapy, CRISPR gene editing, new drugs like crizanlizumab and voxelotor, and advances in bone marrow transplantation are reshaping what's possible.

Early detection, personalized medicine, and global advocacy are also helping more people live longer, healthier lives.

While access and affordability remain challenges, the progress being made shows that change is coming. For the first time in history, we are looking at potential cures—not just treatments.

Here are some developments that could shape the future of sickle cell disease:

1. Gene Therapy and Gene Editing

- Gene Therapy: One of the most groundbreaking advancements for sickle cell disease is gene therapy. The goal of gene therapy is to correct the underlying genetic mutation that causes sickle cell disease, essentially offering a potential cure.

  Several approaches are being explored:

- Gene Addition: This approach involves inserting a healthy version of the hemoglobin gene into a patient's stem cells. These modified cells are then reintroduced into the patient, where they can produce normal hemoglobin.

- Gene Editing (CRISPR-Cas9): A revolutionary technique like CRISPR-Cas9 is being used to edit the genes of a patient's stem cells. This technique specifically targets the sickle cell mutation and corrects it at the DNA level, offering the potential to create long-term or permanent cures. Trials using CRISPR technology, such as the one used to edit the "BCL11A" gene to reactivate fetal hemoglobin production, have shown promise in clinical settings.

- Progress in Clinical Trials: Early trials of gene therapy have already shown success in reducing symptoms, and in some cases, offering long-term relief from the disease. Some patients have achieved normal or near-normal hemoglobin levels after undergoing gene therapy. While these treatments are still in the trial phase, the progress is very promising.

- Challenges and Costs: While gene therapies are showing great potential, they are still in early stages and can be costly, with prices ranging from several hundred thousand to over a million dollars per patient. Additionally, long-term effects and safety need more research. However, these technologies are expected to improve over time, making them more accessible and effective.

2. New Medications and Treatments

- Hydroxyurea: Hydroxyurea has been the gold standard for treating sickle cell disease, but new advancements aim to build upon or improve upon it.

Research is ongoing to develop more effective and personalized medications that can:

- Increase the production of fetal hemoglobin (which does not sickle), thereby reducing sickling of red blood cells.
- Improve red blood cell quality and reduce the frequency of pain crises and complications.

Crizanlizumab and Voxelotor: These two new drugs have already been approved in some regions to treat sickle cell disease:

- Crizanlizumab: This drug is a monoclonal antibody that helps reduce pain crises by preventing red blood cells from sticking to blood vessel walls. It has shown effectiveness in reducing the frequency of pain crises in clinical trials.
- Voxelotor: This drug works by increasing the amount of oxygen carried by sickled red blood cells, reducing the polymerization that leads to sickling. It has been shown to improve hemoglobin levels and reduce complications associated with sickle cell disease.

Pain Management: For patients with chronic pain, including pain crises, new therapies are being researched to better manage pain. These include non-opioid medications, more advanced pain management techniques, and individualized approaches tailored to the patient's needs.

3. Bone Marrow and Stem Cell Transplantation

- Stem Cell Transplantation: Stem cell or bone marrow transplants remain one of the most effective treatment options for sickle cell disease, offering the possibility of a cure. However, this treatment is not suitable for everyone, as it requires a close match from a donor (usually a sibling). Additionally, it carries significant risks, such as graft-versus-host disease (GVHD), where the transplanted cells attack the patient's body.

- Haploidentical Transplant: Recent advancements in stem cell transplantation have explored haploidentical transplants (using a parent as the donor) to overcome some of the limitations of donor matching. This approach has shown promise and is being studied in clinical trials.

- Gene-modified Stem Cell Transplant: Research is also focusing on modifying a patient's own stem cells to make them less likely to sickle, which would reduce the need for a donor altogether. This approach, coupled with gene editing, is being tested in clinical trials.

4. Improved Screening and Early Detection

- Newborn Screening: Many countries have now implemented newborn screening programs that test infants for sickle cell disease shortly after birth. Early detection allows for earlier intervention, helping to reduce the severity of the disease and the risk of complications. Newborn screening programs are being expanded globally, especially in areas where sickle cell disease is more common, such as Sub-Saharan Africa.

- Expanded Screening: Researchers are also working to develop blood tests and diagnostic tools that can identify early signs of complications, such as stroke or organ damage, before symptoms appear. This would enable doctors to intervene earlier and improve long-term outcomes for patients.

5. Personalized Medicine and Precision Treatment

- Tailored Treatments: As the understanding of sickle cell disease advances, personalized and precision medicine will play an increasingly important role. Researchers are working to understand the genetic and environmental factors that affect how each person with sickle cell experiences the disease. This knowledge will allow for more targeted and effective treatments tailored to an individual's genetic makeup and lifestyle.

- Pharmacogenomics: The study of how genes affect an individual's response to drugs (pharmacogenomics) is also a promising area of research. By using genetic testing, doctors could determine the best treatments or pain management strategies for each patient based on their genetic profile.

6. Global Health Initiatives

- Access to Care: One of the biggest challenges in sickle cell care globally is the lack of access to essential treatments, especially in low- and middle-income countries (LMICs). Programs are being developed to improve access to early diagnosis, affordable treatments, and better healthcare infrastructure in areas where sickle cell is most prevalent, such as in parts of Africa, the Middle East, and India.

- Global Awareness and Advocacy: Increased advocacy and awareness campaigns are helping to shed light on sickle cell disease, reducing stigma and promoting better health care policies. International organizations, such as the World Health Organization (WHO) and the Sickle Cell Disease Association of

America (SCDAA), are actively involved in raising awareness and improving care globally.

7. Improved Management of Complications

- Managing Organ Damage: Sickle cell disease can lead to organ damage (e.g., in the kidneys, lungs, heart, and spleen), but advancements in imaging, monitoring, and preventive care are improving how these complications are managed. New drugs and treatments that target organ damage and prevent complications, like stroke and acute chest syndrome, are being developed.

- Better Pain Management: Pain management continues to be a critical aspect of sickle cell disease care. Research into non-opioid pain treatments, pain prevention strategies, and personalized approaches to managing chronic pain are making it easier for patients to lead active, healthy lives.

8. Patient Empowerment and Education

- Self-Management Tools: Advances in technology are providing patients with better tools to manage their condition. Mobile health apps and wearable devices that track pain, hydration, medications, and symptoms can help patients stay on top of their health and communicate more effectively with their healthcare providers.

- Telemedicine: Telemedicine is becoming more widely used for routine check-ups and consultations, making it easier for patients to access care without having to travel. This is especially important for individuals living in remote areas or those with limited access to specialized care.

The future of sickle cell disease holds incredible promise. From gene therapies that may one day offer a cure, to new medications that improve quality of life, the landscape is rapidly evolving.

While challenges remain, particularly around access to care, these advancements offer hope for individuals living with sickle cell disease and their families. The ongoing research, global efforts to increase awareness, and strides in patient-centered care suggest that a future with better outcomes and even potential cures is on the horizon.

🐾 Pause & Reflect

Future of Sickle Cell Treatments

How does it feel to think about a future where SCD might be cured?

Does it fill you with hope, fear, or both?

Write down your feelings honestly—you don't need to filter them.

Part IX: Mastering the Healthcare Maze
📖 Reflection | Affirmation | Prayer | Action

Reflection: Your Healthcare Story

Look back on your healthcare experiences—the good and the hard.

1. What moments made you feel truly heard and respected?
2. When did you feel dismissed or overlooked?
3. If you could speak to your past self walking into that hospital or clinic, what would you say?

Write one sentence of encouragement to carry into your next appointment:

"I am my best advocate. My voice matters. I deserve care and respect."

Affirmation: I Am My Strongest Advocate

- "I come prepared.
- I ask questions.
- I own my health journey with confidence.
- I have the right to be heard, to understand, and to receive compassionate care.
- My experience is valid, and my voice is powerful."

Prayer: Guide Me Through My Healthcare Journey

Dear God, When I walk into the unknown halls of hospitals and clinics, I ask for Your presence. Calm my fears and give me clarity. Help me to speak with confidence and listen with discernment.

Lead me to caregivers who will see me as whole and honor my story. Give me patience when the system feels slow or unfair. Strengthen me to advocate for myself with grace and courage.

Remind me always that I am not alone—you are my healer and helper. Amen.

Action Steps: Prepare for Your Next Appointment

1. Create a "Doctor Visit" Sheet

- List current symptoms, questions, medications, and concerns.
- Bring this sheet with you to every visit.

2. Keep a Log

- Track new treatments, pain episodes, side effects, or changes in your condition.

3. Ask for Clarity

Don't hesitate to say:

- "Can I record this conversation for clarity?"
- "Can you explain that again in simpler terms?"
- "What are my next steps?"

4. Plan Your Support

- Bring a trusted friend or family member if possible for emotional support and note-taking.

Gentle Reminder:

Your healthcare journey is your story to tell—and you deserve to be heard every step of the way.

Preparation and self-advocacy are tools of empowerment, not burden. You are worthy of care, respect, and healing.

Part X: Thriving Beyond the Diagnosis

Chapter 47: Working with Chronic Illness

Okay, y'all, let's be real. I'm going to start this chapter with a confession: I completely failed at working while chronically ill. And by "failed," I mean I worked myself straight into the hospital for over three weeks, with zero job protection, and ended up feeling like the world had handed me a big ol' "Nope" stamp.

This was my reality in 2021, and honestly, I wouldn't wish it on anyone. But here's the thing—we can learn from it.

So, let's talk about working while sick and what you can do to avoid making the same mistakes I did (trust me, you don't want to repeat them).

Back then, I wasn't just battling fatigue and pain from sickle cell anemia—pneumonia decided to join the party too.

Picture this: I'm gasping for air, juggling life as a homeschooling mom, a full-time nursing student, managing a household, and working full-time midnight shifts as a sterile processing technician. Sleep?

Apparently optional.

Financial stress? Check. Emotional chaos? Double check. Add in a toxic relationship filled with infidelity and disrespect, and my body finally said, "Hold my oxygen mask," landing me in the hospital with acute chest syndrome.

So yeah—thriving wasn't exactly the word I'd use for that season.

Here's the kicker: my employer had no idea I had sickle cell anemia. And no, I'm not saying they should have magically known, but here's the truth—if I had disclosed my illness and filed Family Medical Leave Act (FMLA) paperwork, I would have had job security.

FMLA would have protected me during my absences. Instead, every sick day looked like a mystery. No documentation, no explanation, just a "flaky" employee who kept disappearing. That lack of protection cost me both my health and my job.

And unfortunately, that wasn't the first time. A similar situation previously happened when my sister, Erica, became critically ill. She was airlifted to the University of Michigan in Ann Arbor with an unidentified infection and collapsed lungs.

As her guardian I spent weeks driving back and forth, Pontiac to Ann Arbor, sometimes staying at the hospital for days on end. Later, the same crazy rountine when my son needed serious hospital care. He spent a total of eight months in NICU (neonatal intensive care unit).

In both cases, I had no FMLA or workplace accommodations in place. My absences weren't seen as love and caregiving—they looked like irresponsibility. Eventually, the pressure became too much, and I had to leave those jobs as well.

Here's the lesson: no matter whether it's for yourself or someone you love, having the right protections at work is a game-changer.

Don't wait until you're in a hospital bed or at your loved one's side to start thinking about your rights.

Learn about FMLA and other workplace protections now. They may feel like a hassle to set up, but they can mean the difference between keeping your job and losing everything you've worked for.

Balancing work with a chronic illness isn't easy. It requires support, flexibility, and understanding—from your employer, from your coworkers, and most importantly, from yourself. So, take care of your health, your family, and your employment too. Because protecting your future is just as important as surviving the present.

Here's some help on how to navigate it:

- Know Your Rights in the Workplace: In many countries, including the U.S., laws like the Americans with Disabilities Act (ADA) protect individuals with chronic conditions. Understand your right to request accommodations such as more flexible hours, a chair for rest breaks, or permission to work from home when necessary.

- Communicate with Your Employer: It's important to have an honest conversation with your employer about your condition. A doctor's note can be helpful to clarify your needs without going into extensive detail about your health.

- Take Care of Yourself: Working while ill can be exhausting. Don't feel guilty about needing rest. Your health should always come first. You may need to adjust your work hours or job duties as your health fluctuates.

Some People with sickle cell anemia or other chronic illnesses often face several significant hurdles when trying to maintain a full-time job.

Some of these challenges include:

1. **Frequent medical appointments**

Individuals may need to attend regular doctor visits, receive treatments, or undergo tests. These appointments can conflict with work schedules, requiring time off or flexible hours.

2. **Physical limitations and fatigue**

Chronic illnesses, such as sickle cell anemia, can cause extreme fatigue, pain crises, and other symptoms that can make it difficult to maintain energy and focus throughout the day.

3. **Unpredictable flare-ups**

With conditions like sickle cell anemia, flare-ups or complications (e.g., pain crises) can be sudden and severe, leading to unplanned absences or a decrease in productivity during the workday.

4. **Discrimination and stigma**

Unfortunately, some people with chronic illnesses face discrimination in the workplace due to misconceptions about their condition or its impact on work performance. This can result in fewer opportunities for career advancement or even employment termination.

5. **Lack of workplace accommodations**:

Many individuals with chronic illnesses require accommodations such as flexible work hours, the ability to work from home, or ergonomic changes to their workspace. Not all employers provide or understand the need for these adjustments.

6. **Cognitive impairments**

Some chronic illnesses can affect cognitive function, leading to memory problems, difficulty concentrating, or brain fog. This can hinder a person's ability to perform tasks that require sustained focus or problem-solving.

7. **Mental health challenges**

The stress of managing a chronic illness, combined with concerns about job security, financial stability, and social isolation, can lead to anxiety, depression, or burnout. These mental health challenges can further complicate their ability to work full-time.

8. **Physical strain and exhaustion**

Long hours or physically demanding work may worsen symptoms, causing more pain or discomfort. The inability to sustain physical activity for long periods can hinder productivity and lead to absenteeism.

9. **Lack of awareness or understanding**

In some cases, colleagues or employers may not fully understand the nature of chronic illnesses, leading to feelings of isolation or frustration when it comes to explaining one's needs or limitations.

Here's the lesson: whether for your health or for a loved one's, get protections in place before crisis hits.

Learn your rights, file the paperwork, and don't wait until you're in a hospital bed to advocate for yourself.

🦬 Reflection | Affirmation | Prayer | Action
Working with Chronic Illness

Reflection
- Have you told your employer or school about your chronic illness? Why or why not?
- What fears hold you back from asking for accommodations or protections?
- Imagine the relief you'd feel if you had safeguards in place. What one step can you take this week to start that process?

Affirmation
"I am worthy of protection. My health and my work both matter."

Prayer
Lord, give me courage to speak truthfully about my needs and wisdom to know when and how to share them. Help me to see myself not as a burden, but as someone valuable, capable, and deserving of support.

Action
- Learn about your rights (FMLA, ADA, or equivalent).
- If safe, begin the paperwork or schedule a conversation with HR.
- Write down one accommodation that would make your work life healthier.

Chapter 48: Workplace Support & Accommodations

Working with chronic illness can feel like walking a tightrope—balancing pain, exhaustion, and responsibilities while trying to hold onto your job. But one thing I've learned? Having allies at work can literally save your life.

I'll never forget sitting on the curb outside work in 2021, too sick to walk inside. My supervisor, Olivia, didn't brush me off—she listened, called paramedics, and ran across the skywalk to reach me. That decision, that compassion, likely saved my life.

Working while dealing with life and managing a chronic illness is incredibly challenging. Every day can feel like a balancing act between pushing through pain and holding onto your job.

But here's something I learned the hard way: the more people who understand what you're going through, the better it can be for you. Having allies and support in the workplace can be life changing—literally.

In 2021. I was sick—really sick—but still trying to work. It got so bad one day that I called in from the curb outside my job's entrance because I couldn't even make it inside. I was exhausted, out of breath, and trying to convince myself I just needed sleep.

Thankfully, I had a supervisor, Olivia, who I trusted enough to tell what was going on. She didn't brush it off—she listened and told me I sounded like I needed to go to the emergency room. I told her no, I'd just sit on the curb, catch my breath, and go home. I was beyond tired, y'all. But she was smart—and compassionate.

While we were still on the phone, I looked up and saw her running across our job's skywalk toward me. She had already called the paramedics to meet me in the employee parking lot. To this day, I thank God for her. Because if I had gone home to sleep like I planned, I may not have woken up.

Turns out I had double pneumonia turned to acute chest syndrome. I ended up in the hospital for weeks, but I got the treatment I needed—because someone at work was looking out for me when I wasn't even looking out for myself.

So let me say this: don't make the same mistake I did. Don't suffer in silence. Tell the right people what's going on. Let someone be there for you when you can't be there for yourself.

That brings us to a key question: how can someone build that kind of support at work? How do you form allies who understand and are ready to help when things get hard?

It starts with communication. Being open with your supervisors, coworkers, and even HR about what you're facing helps them better understand your needs.

This creates space for real support—and real solutions—so that people with chronic illnesses like sickle cell anemia can thrive, even in the workplace.

Here are some strategies that may help:

1. Open and Honest Communication

- Be transparent: It's important to communicate openly with your boss or HR about your condition, how it affects your work, and any accommodations that might be helpful. You don't need to share all the medical details, but providing enough information about your limitations or symptoms can foster understanding.

- Clarify your needs: Explain specific needs or adjustments, such as flexible working hours, time for medical appointments, or the ability to work from home when necessary. Be clear about how these adjustments can help you stay productive and contribute to the team.

2. Educate and Raise Awareness

- Provide information: Share reputable resources or medical documents that explain your condition. This can help demystify your illness and reduce stigma. You might offer to help your team learn more if they are open to it.

- Offer a quick explanation: For colleagues who may not fully understand, provide a simple and easy-to-understand explanation of how your condition affects your work, making it clear that you're committed to doing your job to the best of your ability.

3. Document Your Needs and Accommodations

- Create a formal plan: If needed, work with HR to create a formal accommodation plan. This ensures your needs are clear and in writing, helping avoid misunderstandings or miscommunications down the road.

- Regular updates: Keep your employer informed of any changes in your health that may affect your work. This helps maintain a dialogue and ensures that any adjustments are up to date.

4. Set Realistic Expectations

- Be realistic about your limitations: You know your body best. Set realistic expectations for what you can achieve on a typical day, and what might be a stretch for you. For example, if you're experiencing fatigue, let your boss know in advance if you might need a lighter workload or extra time to complete a task.

- Plan for flare-ups: If you anticipate a potential flare-up or health issue, try to plan ahead (if possible). For example, if you need time off for a medical procedure, request time off in advance to minimize disruption.

5. Be Flexible and Collaborative

- Work with your employer: Employers often appreciate employees who show flexibility and a willingness to find solutions that work for everyone. Be open to discussing possible accommodations, like a flexible work schedule or changing tasks to fit your physical limitations.

- Offer solutions: If you need accommodations, propose solutions that could work for both you and the company. For example, you could suggest altering deadlines or rotating tasks that may require physical exertion.

6. Use Available Resources

- Know your rights: Familiarize yourself with the laws and policies related to workplace accommodations, such as the Americans with Disabilities Act (ADA) or any applicable local regulations. This can help you advocate for yourself and understand your rights.

- Seek support from HR: If you feel comfortable, involve Human Resources early on in your discussions, especially if you need formal accommodations. HR can help you navigate workplace policies and advocate for necessary adjustments.

7. Manage Your Health Proactively

- Take care of your health: By proactively managing your health, such as keeping medical appointments, following treatment plans, and practicing self-care, you can demonstrate that you're doing your part to stay well and minimize disruptions.

- Have backup plans: Consider having a backup plan in place for when you're not feeling well. For example, having a colleague who can step in temporarily, or ensuring that tasks can be handed over quickly if you need to take unplanned time off, helps reduce strain on the team.

8. Be Professional and Demonstrate Reliability

- Stay committed to your role: Despite the challenges, show that you are committed to doing your best. When possible, meet deadlines and show your dedication to your work. This can help build trust with your employer and coworkers.

- Manage your time effectively: Focus on time management strategies to balance work with self-care, especially when energy levels are low.

9. Seek Support from Colleagues

- Build a supportive network: If you feel comfortable, consider educating a few trusted colleagues about your condition. Having allies at work can help create a more supportive work environment.

- Encourage empathy and inclusivity: Foster a workplace culture of inclusivity by encouraging empathy. This can make it easier for others to understand and support you when necessary.

By being proactive, transparent, and collaborative, individuals with chronic illnesses can build an understanding, supportive work environment.

The goal is to work with your employer and colleagues to create a setting where you can contribute effectively while managing your health.

So, hear me: don't suffer in silence.

Tell someone you trust what's going on. Build support before crisis comes.

🕊 Reflection | Affirmation | Prayer | Action
Workplace Support & Accommodations

Reflection

- Who in your workplace (or school) can you trust with your truth?
- What keeps you from sharing your needs openly?

Affirmation

"I am worthy of support. I do not carry this alone."

Prayer

God, thank You for people like Olivia who show up with compassion and courage. Bring trustworthy allies into my life. Give me discernment about who to confide in, and boldness to ask for help when I need it. Amen

Action

- Identify one ally at work or school to share your needs with.
- Write down one specific accommodation that would help you thrive.
- Keep a short "health script" ready—simple words to explain your needs when urgency makes it hard.

Chapter 49: Maintaining Work

Balancing employment with chronic illness can feel overwhelming—but stability is possible. Flexibility, accommodations, disability benefits, and alternative work paths are real tools that can help.

You don't have to fit into the box of a "traditional" 9-to-5 to be successful. Whether it's part-time, remote work, freelancing, or even starting your own business, your path can look different—and still be fulfilling.

Here are some things to consider:

1. Consider Flexible or Remote Work

- Freelancing/Contract work: Depending on your skills, freelancing or contract work can provide the flexibility to work when you're feeling well and take time off when needed. This could include jobs like writing, graphic design, programming, virtual assistance, or consulting.

- Remote jobs: Many companies offer remote or hybrid roles that allow for flexibility in work hours and location. Remote work may help manage fatigue or the need to rest when necessary.

- Part-time roles: A part-time position might provide a better work-life balance and reduce the pressure of full-time commitments while still earning an income.

2. Look into Disability Benefits

- Short-Term or Long-Term Disability: If you're unable to work consistently, you might qualify for short-term or long-term disability insurance. If you have coverage through your employer or a private plan, this could offer some financial support while you focus on your health.

- Social Security Disability Insurance (SSDI): In some cases, individuals with chronic conditions like sickle cell anemia may qualify for SSDI if their illness significantly limits their ability to work. The application process can be lengthy and complex, but it's worth looking into if your condition is severely affecting your ability to maintain a job.
- Supplemental Security Income (SSI): If your condition prevents you from working and you have limited income or resources, you may be eligible for SSI benefits.

3. Workplace Accommodations

- Request accommodations: If you haven't already, you may want to explore reasonable workplace accommodations under laws such as the Americans with Disabilities Act (ADA). Accommodations might include flexible work hours, working from home, or reducing the physical demands of your job.
- Part-time or reduced hours: If full-time work is too demanding, you may be able to request reduced hours, modified schedules, or changes to your workload. It's often easier to maintain a steady job if you can scale back your hours to match your energy.

4. Evaluate Vocational Rehabilitation Services

- Many states and organizations offer vocational rehabilitation services to help people with chronic conditions transition into new types of work that may be more manageable. These services may provide job training, career counseling, or job placement support for individuals with disabilities or health concerns.

5. Create a Financial Safety Net

- Emergency savings: If possible, try to build an emergency savings fund to provide financial security during times when you're unable to work. This can ease the financial burden when health issues prevent consistent employment.

- Side hustles or passive income: If health permits, you might consider developing side income streams, such as selling products online, investing, or creating digital content that earns passive income over time.

6. Explore Job Options with Less Physical Demands

- Non-physical roles: If your health condition is causing physical limitations, consider jobs that have less physical strain. For instance, administrative roles, customer service, or data entry positions may be easier to manage.

- Shift in career: You may need to consider retraining for a different field with more flexibility or less physical exertion. Many online courses or certifications can help pivot to a new career that's more manageable.

7. Develop a Support Network

- Professional support: Reach out to career coaches, counselors, or disability advocates who specialize in helping people with chronic illnesses navigate employment challenges. They can provide guidance on finding jobs that suit your needs, understanding your legal rights, and making career transitions.

- Personal support: Having a strong personal support system, including family, friends, and healthcare providers, can make it easier to manage the emotional and practical challenges of navigating employment with a chronic illness.

8. Understand Your Rights and Protections

- Know your rights: In many countries, there are protections in place for people with chronic illnesses or disabilities. These laws often require employers to make reasonable accommodations to help you stay employed. Familiarize yourself with your rights under the Americans with Disabilities Act (ADA) in the U.S., or similar laws in other countries.
- Employment protections: In some cases, your job cannot be terminated solely due to health-related absences or condition-related limitations. Knowing these protections can help you advocate for yourself at work and protect against unfair treatment.

9. Consider Self-Employment

- Entrepreneurship: If consistent employment is too difficult, you might consider starting your own business, either full-time or part-time. Owning a business or being self-employed allows for greater flexibility and control over your schedule, workload, and work environment. It might also provide a chance to pursue a passion or interest that aligns with your health capacity.

10. Explore Community and Social Services

- Charitable organizations: Investigate local or national organizations that offer financial assistance, grants, or programs specifically for individuals with chronic illnesses. Some nonprofits provide support with medical costs, rent, and other expenses, especially for those unable to work.

- Health insurance assistance: If you struggle to afford medical insurance or treatment, research programs that aid people with chronic illnesses. Some companies offer special assistance programs that may help offset medical costs while you're not working full-time.

11. Maintain a Healthy Balance

Focus on self-care: Prioritize your physical and mental health by practicing self-care routines that help you manage your chronic illness, reduce stress, and stay as healthy as possible. This may include regular doctor visits, medication management, exercise, and relaxation techniques to prevent flare-ups.

Pause & Reflect – Maintaining Work

- What would "sustainable work" look like for you—not based on others' expectations, but on your health and your season of life?
- Which adjustments (big or small) could make work more manageable right now?
- Are you open to redefining success if it means more stability and health?

Chapter 50: College & Career with Chronic Illness

Education and career don't have to stop because of chronic illness. Your path may look different, but it's still yours. Flexibility, resilience, and support systems can help you reach your goals in your own way and timing.

Whether you choose part-time classes, online learning, or shift into a new career, you are building a future that works with your illness, not against it.

This chapter will guide you through:

- Choosing a flexible academic path that supports your health
- Managing your energy and time effectively as a student and mother
- Financial planning for education and healthcare
- Building a supportive network that lifts you up
- Cultivating the resilience to keep going, even on the hard days

Remember, you can create a life that works with your illness—not in spite of it.

Let this chapter be your companion as you move forward with confidence, grace, and determination.

Tips for college & career success:

1. Embrace Flexibility: Tailoring Your College Experience

- Choose Online or Hybrid Programs: Many universities offer online or hybrid options, which allow for flexibility in attending classes and managing health needs. Look for accredited institutions with these offerings.

- Part-Time Enrollment: Consider attending part-time if full-time coursework feels overwhelming. This can ease the load and prevent burnout. Many schools have options for part-time students to access financial aid.

- Accommodation for Health Needs: Work with your school's disability services to set up necessary accommodations, such as extended deadlines or adjusted exam times. Don't hesitate to ask for help when needed.

- Prioritize Self-Care: Make sure to schedule self-care into your academic calendar. Prioritize sleep, nutrition, hydration, and stress management. This will keep you energized for both school and life as a mother.

2. Managing Energy and Health During College

- Plan Your Schedule Wisely: Space out your classes to avoid overloading yourself. Aim for a balance of in-person and online courses that don't demand long hours on campus daily.

- Communicate with Professors: Be proactive in communicating your health challenges with professors. Most educators will be understanding and

willing to provide flexibility when informed in advance.
- Utilize Campus Resources: Many schools have counseling services, health centers, and support groups specifically designed to assist students dealing with chronic illnesses. Take full advantage of these resources to manage your health and mental well-being.

3. Time Management for Single Mothers

- Set Realistic Goals: Break tasks into smaller, manageable chunks. Use a planner or digital calendar to stay on top of assignments, deadlines, and other responsibilities.
- Delegate When Possible: Rely on friends, family, or other trusted individuals to help with childcare when needed, allowing you to focus on studying or taking care of yourself.
- Use Technology for Support: Leverage apps and tools for studying, organizing tasks, and keeping track of deadlines. Tools like Trello, Google Calendar, or Evernote can be lifesaving when balancing school and motherhood.

4. Choosing the Right Career: Sustainable and Fulfilling Options

- Assess Your Strengths and Interests: Identify careers that align with your passions and strengths, not just those that are high paying. A career you find meaningful will help you maintain motivation through tough times.
- Consider Flexible or Remote Jobs: Look for fields that offer flexibility, such as remote work or freelancing.

- Careers in tech, writing, marketing, consulting, or customer service often have more adaptable work arrangements.

- Think Long-Term Sustainability: With chronic illness, it's important to consider a career that is sustainable in the long term. Choose one that offers flexibility in hours, location, and work demands, as well as room for advancement.

- Look into Disability-Friendly Careers: Some industries, such as healthcare, counseling, and social services, offer positions that are well-suited for individuals with chronic illness. These fields often have flexible work options and can also provide a fulfilling way to help others facing similar challenges.

- Evaluate Job Benefits: When selecting a career, consider the healthcare benefits and insurance options available through employers. Jobs that offer robust health coverage will significantly ease your financial burden as you manage your illness.

5. Financial Planning for Education and Career Success

- Scholarships and Financial Aid: Investigate scholarship programs designed specifically for students with chronic illnesses or single mothers. Many institutions offer financial aid, and there are also external organizations that provide grants and scholarships for students in need.

- Plan for Healthcare Costs: Ensure your career path includes access to quality healthcare. Research job options that provide strong health insurance benefits or that are compatible with your personal healthcare needs.

- Build a Safety Net: It's important to have a financial cushion, especially when living with a chronic illness. Create an emergency fund that can cover unforeseen medical expenses or times when you may need to take time off from work.

6. Cultivating a Support Network

- Connect with Others in Similar Situations: Look for online communities or local groups for single mothers or those living with chronic illness. These communities can provide emotional support, practical advice, and networking opportunities.

- Lean on Family and Friends: Don't hesitate to ask for help. Whether it's watching your children for a few hours or helping with household chores, your loved ones want to support you.

- Find a Mentor: Seek out mentors in your desired field who understand the unique challenges of balancing chronic illness, motherhood, and professional aspirations. They can provide guidance, emotional support, and insight into career advancement.

7. Fostering Resilience and Persistence

- Stay Patient with Yourself: Progress in education and career will take time. Celebrate small victories and don't be too hard on yourself if you encounter setbacks. Your resilience and determination will take you far.

- Practice Self-Compassion: Acknowledge the effort you're putting into both your education and career. You are doing an incredible job balancing these priorities, and it's okay to have moments of struggle.

- Stay Flexible: Life with chronic illness can be unpredictable. Learn to embrace adaptability and resilience, knowing that some days may be harder than others. Prioritize your well-being and allow yourself room to adjust when necessary.

Pursuing higher education and a fulfilling career as a mother living with chronic illness is entirely achievable with the right mindset and strategies.

By planning carefully, leveraging support, and choosing a career that aligns with your personal needs and goals, you can thrive academically, professionally, and personally.

Always remember to give yourself grace as you move forward, and embrace the journey with courage and resilience.

🦋 Reflection| Affirmation | Prayer | Action
College & Career with Chronic Illness

Reflection
- What are your dreams for education or career right now?
- Where do you feel fear or limitation?

Affirmation
"My illness shapes my path, but it does not define my destination."

Prayer
Lord, guide my steps in education and career. Help me see possibilities, not just limitations. Give me courage to pursue what aligns with both my health and Your purpose.

Action
- Write down one next step toward your educational or career goal.
- Research scholarships, flexible programs, or career paths that fit your season.
- Share your dream with someone who can encourage or mentor you.

Chapter 51: Travel Tips for SCD Warriors

Travel opens the door to new experiences, perspectives, and possibilities. Travel can also feel intimidating with sickle cell disease, but it is possible—and even joyful—with preparation. By planning ahead, carrying medications, hydrating, and pacing yourself, you can explore the world safely.

Travel isn't about pushing your body—it's about experiencing freedom and joy while respecting your limits.

Understanding Common Travel Concerns

People living with SCD often face added anxieties when preparing for a trip.

Recognizing these common concerns is the first step toward managing them effectively:

- Pain Crises: Sudden episodes can be triggered by dehydration, cold exposure, high altitudes, or physical stress.
- Limited Access to Medical Care: Fear of being far from familiar doctors or emergency services.
- Medication Challenges: Concerns about carrying enough medicine, passing through customs, or filling prescriptions abroad.
- Travel Delays: Disruptions can lead to exhaustion or missed medication schedules.
- Temperature Extremes: Cold or hot climates may aggravate symptoms or provoke a crisis.

- Increased Risk of Infection: Exposure to unfamiliar pathogens, especially in crowded or unsanitary environments.

Awareness of these risks makes it easier to take proactive, protective steps.

Here are the top 10 Travel Tips for Sickle Cell Warriors

1. Consult Your Healthcare Provider Early

Schedule a pre-travel check-up. Ask for advice tailored to your itinerary, and obtain a medical letter describing your condition and prescribed medications.

2. Always Keep Medications Accessible

Pack all essential medications in your carry-on bag. Bring more than you need in case of travel delays, and keep medications in their original labeled containers.

3. Hydrate Consistently

Dehydration is a major trigger for SCD-related complications. Drink plenty of water before, during, and after travel—especially on flights. Avoid alcohol and caffeine.

4. Dress Smartly for Comfort and Climate

Wear breathable, loose-fitting clothing to promote circulation. Layer up in colder climates, and don't forget sun protection in hot or tropical destinations.

5. Purchase Travel Insurance That Covers Pre-Existing Conditions

Make sure your policy includes emergency medical care, hospital stays, and repatriation if needed.

6. **Know Where to Get Medical Help at Your Destination**

Research hospitals, urgent care centers, and pharmacies ahead of time. Have emergency numbers saved in your phone and printed in your travel documents.

7. **Build Rest into Your Schedule**

Avoid overexertion. Leave space in your itinerary to rest and recover—especially after long travel days.

8. **Manage Temperature Sensitivity**

Use heat packs in cold environments or cooling towels in hot ones. Adjust your clothing and environment to stay comfortable.

9. **Pay Attention to Early Warning Signs**

Act quickly at the first sign of fatigue, dehydration, or a developing pain crisis. Use your medications, rest, and seek help if symptoms worsen.

10. **Explore Comfortable Travel Alternatives**

If flying is stressful or physically taxing, consider alternatives like train or car travel, which may offer greater control and flexibility.

Travel with Chronic Illness
Reflection| Affirmation | Prayer | Action

Reflection
- Where is one place you've dreamed of traveling?
- What steps would make that trip feel safe and possible for you?
- How could travel—even local or small—remind you that your life is bigger than your diagnosis?

Affirmation

"I am free to explore the world on my terms. Preparation and wisdom are my travel companions."

Prayer

God, thank You for the beauty of this world. Give me wisdom to prepare well and courage to step out in joy. Protect me in every journey and remind me that my diagnosis does not cancel my dreams.

Action
- Choose one trip (big or small) to plan this year.
- Complete the "SCD Warrior Travel Checklist."
- Share your plan with a travel buddy who can support you.

SCD Warrior Travel Checklist

Before You Travel

- Talk to your doctor about your travel plans
- Get a signed medical letter and emergency care instructions
- Request any necessary vaccines or preventive medications
- Pack a medical alert bracelet, if you have one
- Purchase comprehensive travel insurance
- Make digital and paper copies of your passport, prescriptions, and insurance documents
- Research local hospitals, clinics, and emergency numbers

Medications & Supplies

- Pack all prescriptions in labeled, original containers
- Bring enough medication for the full trip—plus extra
- Include over-the-counter pain relievers, hydration powders, heat/cold packs
- Prepare a small travel medical kit for emergencies

During Travel

- Stay well hydrated (especially during air travel)
- Carry a reusable water bottle and refill often
- Dress in layers, bring a jacket or blanket for cold flights
- Stretch or walk every 1–2 hours on long journeys

- Avoid alcohol and caffeinated drinks
- Keep medications and your health letter accessible

At Your Destination

- Balance activity with plenty of rest
- Monitor for signs of pain, dehydration, or fatigue
- Stick to your medication schedule and hydration routine
- Know where to go for emergency care
- Don't hesitate to ask for help or explain your condition when needed

Pro Tips from SCD Warriors

- Choose aisle seats for easier movement on planes
- Bring comfort items—like a travel pillow, blanket, and snacks
- Avoid high-altitude or extreme-weather destinations if they are known triggers
- Practice stress management techniques—deep breathing, stretching, or light meditation
- Advocate for yourself confidently—you are your best health advocate

Living with sickle cell disease means adapting to life with care and foresight—but it should never mean giving up your dreams of exploration. With thoughtful preparation and self-awareness, the world is absolutely within reach.

You are strong. You are wise. And you are free to travel on your terms.

Part X: Thriving Beyond the Diagnosis
Reflection | Affirmation | Prayer | Action

Reflection
- Looking back at this section, which area feels most urgent for you right now—work, school, career, or travel?
- Where do you sense God inviting you to choose wisdom over striving?
- What new opportunities do you feel hopeful about, even with the reality of chronic illness?

Affirmation
"I am more than my diagnosis. I am capable, worthy, and equipped to thrive in every area of my life."

Prayer
Lord, thank You for reminding me that life is still full of possibility. Teach me to balance wisdom with courage, rest with perseverance, and planning with faith. Guide me in my work, studies, travels, and dreams, so that I may walk in freedom, strength, and hope.

Action
- Choose one step this week (big or small) toward thriving—whether filling out workplace paperwork, researching flexible programs, setting aside travel funds, or simply resting.
- Journal about how your identity is bigger than your illness.
- Share one piece of your journey with someone you trust to build accountability and encouragement.

Part XI: Advocacy and Awareness

Chapter 52: Becoming an Advocate

Advocating for a loved one who lives with a chronic illness involves both emotional support and practical action. Being an advocate for my younger sister and my son has taught me just how powerful that role can be.

I'd like to share an experience when someone advocated for me without a second thought.

During a major hospital stay, I was in the midst of an intense crisis while experiencing acute chest syndrome. A close friend of mine, Kiara, happened to be working on the same hospital floor where I was a patient. She stopped by to check in on me and say hi—and immediately noticed I was in distress.

Kiara quickly spoke to my nurse, who, after assessing me, called in the Rapid Response Team (RRT). They took swift action and stabilized me. Kiara's decision to check in, to speak up, and to act was an incredible example of true care—true advocacy—at a moment when I couldn't advocate for myself.

Having someone step in, speak up, and help carry the load can truly be the difference between life and death.

Through my own experiences as an advocate, I've come to understand how essential this role is. Sometimes, we become advocates by default—but even then, it can be one of the most rewarding and meaningful things we do.

Whether it's picking up groceries, managing medications, or sitting bedside during doctor's appointments, every act of support matters. Advocacy isn't just about emergencies or hospital visits—it's also about the daily check-ins: "Did you eat?" "Did you take your meds?" "How are you really feeling today?"

Showing up in small, consistent ways is a powerful form of love. Helping your loved one feel seen, heard, and cared for gives them strength—and helps you build a deeper bond.

Here are some practical steps to help you step into this role with confidence:

Steps to Becoming an Advocate

1. Listen and Understand

Take the time to really listen to their needs, frustrations, and experiences. Understanding their condition and how it affects them daily is key to being an effective advocate.

2. Educate Yourself

Learn about the illness—its symptoms, treatments, and possible complications. This will allow you to support them better and help communicate their needs with healthcare providers, family, or friends.

3. Help with Medical Appointments

Offer to go with them to doctor visits or treatment sessions. You can help by taking notes, asking questions, and ensuring they understand the information being shared.

4. Stay Organized

Keep a shared calendar, medication list, and document folder (paper or digital). Track symptoms, test results, and important contact information so nothing gets lost in the shuffle.

5. **Communicate with Healthcare Providers**

Sometimes, navigating the healthcare system can be difficult. Help facilitate communication with doctors, nurses, and specialists, ensuring that the person's concerns are heard and addressed.

6. **Advocate for Workplace or School Adjustments**

If their illness impacts their work or schooling, help negotiate accommodations like flexible hours, breaks, or adjusted workloads. Know the rights they have under the law (such as the Americans with Disabilities Act in the U.S.).

7. **Ensure Emotional Support**

Chronic illness can be isolating, so offer a listening ear, encourage them to express their feelings, and be there when they need comfort or distraction.

8. **Research Treatment Options**

Help research treatment plans or alternative therapies that could improve their quality of life, but always ensure that medical decisions are made in consultation with healthcare providers.

9. **Help with Daily Tasks**

Depending on the severity of the illness, you might need to help with physical tasks such as cooking, cleaning, or running errands. These gestures go a long way in reducing their stress.

10. **Advocate for Financial or Insurance Assistance**

Chronic illness can bring financial strain, so help research financial aid, insurance coverage, or other resources that may help ease the burden.

11. Be Patient and Flexible

Chronic illness often comes with unpredictability. Be prepared to adjust plans, expectations, and routines when needed, and always offer reassurance that you're there for the long haul.

Consistency is the heartbeat of advocacy—and love. But also, watch for burnout. Take care of yourself, too—rest, talk to someone you trust, and allow yourself to be human. Even when things are hard. Even when you feel tired. You don't have to do it all alone. Reach out to other family members, friends, support groups, or professional advocates. It's okay to ask for help.

Above all, remember that your role as an advocate is to empower your loved one while respecting their autonomy and wishes. Your support can be a great comfort as they navigate the complexities of living with a chronic illness.

Pause & Reflect

Becoming an Advocate

- Who in your life has stood up for you in a moment you couldn't speak for yourself?
- Where might you need to step into advocacy for someone you love—or even for yourself?
- What small act of consistency could make the biggest difference this week?

Chapter 53: Advocacy and Education

Your story matters. Speaking up about sickle cell—whether in your family, community, or broader circles—helps spread awareness, break down stigma, and open doors for better care. Advocacy doesn't have to be loud or public; it can start small, with conversations, social media posts, or simply educating those closest to you.

The more people understand sickle cell, the more compassion and support can grow. You have the power to use your voice to create change—not just for yourself but for others who walk this journey too.

🐾 Reflection

- Who in my life could benefit from learning more about sickle cell?
- How might sharing my story help others feel seen or supported?

Affirmation

"My voice matters, and my story can inspire change."

Prayer

Lord, give me boldness to share my story. Use my words to educate, encourage, and advocate for better awareness and care. Amen.

Action

- Share one fact about sickle cell with someone this week.
- Post an encouraging message online to raise awareness.

Chapter 54: Spreading Awareness in Schools & Communities

Raising awareness about sickle cell disease is essential to reducing stigma and increasing understanding. Growing up, there wasn't much information or many resources available for those affected by sickle cell.

My family and I were fortunate to have a sickle cell resource center within walking distance of our home. They provided after school tutoring with snacks, and gave my mother access to resources during a time when we were receiving nearly every form of low-income assistance—DHS, WIC, ADC, Section 8.

One of the highlights of the year was the annual "sickle cell party." Each Christmas, they hosted a celebration for children with sickle cell and their families. There were gifts, food, and so much joy. Those parties made us feel special and seen. When the center moved away, we were deeply saddened, but the impact it had stayed with us. Those experiences gave us joy, connection, and the feeling that we weren't alone.

Today, there are far more resources and information available—but awareness still matters. Every conversation, every event, every post is a chance to shed light and create compassion.

The more people who understand, the more advocates we'll have when support, empathy, and change are needed. Awareness should always be shared in an open, respectful, and informative way.

Ways to Spread Awareness

- Educate Schools: If you're a parent of a child with sickle cell, meet with school staff to ensure your child receives necessary accommodations, such as rest breaks during physical activity or extra time on exams when unwell.

- Community Programs: Launch awareness campaigns or collaborate with local organizations to create educational materials, host events, or organize fundraisers to support families affected by sickle cell.

- Social Media Campaigns: Use platforms like Instagram, Twitter, and Facebook to share facts, personal stories, and helpful resources. Hashtags such as #SickleCellAwareness and #SickleCellWarrior can amplify voices and connect communities.

🦋 Pause & Reflect

Spreading Awareness in Schools & Communities

- What resource, person, or program made a difference for you?

- How could you "pass it on" by creating awareness in your school, church, or community?

- What's one small step you could take to shine light where there's still misunderstanding?

Part XII: Financial and Legal Survival Guide

Chapter 55: Financial Assistance and Resources

There are many financial assistance and resources are available for single mothers and people living with a chronic illness. They can be found on many levels your community your city and there are also government programs. Help is out there for those who need it.

When my life seemed to fall apart in 2021, I reached a breaking point—physically, emotionally, and financially. The stress was overwhelming. But I remember doing two things that started to turn the tide: I prayed, and I planned.

Prayer gave me peace and strength; planning gave me direction. Together, they became the foundation of my journey back toward stability.

And here's what I learned: there is always help—but you must be willing to ask, advocate, and act.

I am grateful for my infusion center and hospital resource center. I confided in a compassionate woman named Ms. P. We talked about all my newfound problems. Going from potentially five figures a month to a negative cash flow was all but debilitating. But her and the resource department was the bridge to a network of support I didn't even know existed.

They helped to connect my family with things we needed—from emotional support services to groceries. That moment taught me a valuable lesson: never suffer in silence. Closed mouths don't get fed.

Ask, Apply, Act

Support won't always come knocking—you must seek it out. I reached out to local agencies and organizations and found assistance for home repairs, utility bills, groceries, and more. But receiving help didn't mean sitting still.

I also took steps on my own by:
- Creating a realistic budget
- Cutting back where I could
- Shopping more strategically
- Applying for every program I qualified for

Slowly but surely, things began to improve. It wasn't instant, but it was progress—and every bit of progress counts.

It Takes Faith and a Plan

Faith without works is dead. So, we pray for help, we ask for help, we apply for help—and while we wait for help, we start helping ourselves.

That means being open, staying informed, and preparing for blessings before they even arrive. We can't always predict life's storms, but we can build our ark in advance.

Practical Financial Support Options

Living with sickle cell (or any chronic illness) can be expensive, but there are resources out there to ease the burden.

Below are some practical steps and support systems you can explore:

1. Government Assistance Programs

Many national and local programs offer financial help for those with chronic conditions:

- Medicaid and Medicare: Offer medical coverage for low-income individuals and those with disabilities.
- Social Security Disability Insurance (SSDI): If your condition prevents you from working, SSDI can provide monthly income.
- Supplemental Security Income (SSI): Offers financial aid to adults and children with disabilities who have limited income.

2. Nonprofits, Charities, and Foundations

Numerous organizations provide direct support, grants, and advocacy for sickle cell patients:

- Sickle Cell Disease Association of America (SCDAA)
- The Assistance Fund
- Health Well Foundation
- Children's Health Insurance Program (CHIP) for families with children

These groups can offer help with medication costs, co-pays, transportation to appointments, and more.

3. Crowdfunding and Community Support

Platforms like GoFundMe and YouCaring have helped many families raise money for medical expenses. Don't be afraid to share your story—people are often more willing to help than you think.

Also, consider:
- Church communities
- Mutual aid groups
- Local food banks
- Women's shelters or family services organizations

Sometimes the help comes from places you least expect.

So even if you're unsure if you'll get approved. you should still apply.

You never know what help may be available to you. Don't deny yourself before you're denied.

In some cases you may not qualify for one program, but you may qualify for another. I remember receiving 15 in food assistance. It wasn't much, but the fact that I received any amount from that agency. Automatically qualified me for benefits to another program. It doesn't hurt you to apply.

Reflection | Affirmation | Prayer | Action

Financial Assistance and Resources

Reflection
- Where in your financial life do you most feel pressure right now?
- How do you usually handle asking for help?

Affirmation
"I am not helpless. I am resourceful, faithful, and worthy of support."

Prayer
Lord, help me to ask boldly, apply faithfully, and act wisely. Remind me that closed mouths don't get fed, and that You've already placed help in my path. Amen

Action
- Apply for one program or grant this week.
- Create a simple written budget to see clearly where your money is going.

Chapter 56: Legal Rights and Protections

Understanding your legal rights is essential for ensuring that you are treated fairly. If you're managing a chronic illness like sickle cell, knowing your rights and understanding your legal options is vital:

- **Workplace Rights**

Laws like the Family and Medical Leave Act (FMLA) and the Americans with Disabilities Act (ADA) protect workers with chronic illnesses. You have the right to request accommodations and time off when needed. If approved, you are protected under these acts, and you may qualify for job accommodations or unpaid leave without penalty.

- **Disability Benefits**

If you are unable to work due to sickle cell, you may qualify for disability benefits. Seek guidance on how to apply for these benefits and what documentation is required.

- **Know your employment rights**

You are protected under the Americans with Disabilities Act (ADA). You may qualify for job accommodations or unpaid leave through the Family and Medical Leave Act (FMLA).

- **Talk to a social worker or legal aid organization**

Many hospitals and nonprofits have legal professionals who can guide you through the system at no cost.

- **Prepare important documents**

Powers of attorney, living wills, and insurance policies should be kept up to date.

As moms, we often feel like we have to hold the world on our shoulders. But thriving with a chronic illness isn't about doing it all—it's about knowing when to pray, when to plan, and when to ask for help. Your strength is not in how much you can carry, but in your ability to build a community, rely on your faith, and use every resource available.

Help is out there. And you are worthy of receiving it.

Pause & Reflect

Legal Rights and Protections

- Which part of legal protection feels most overwhelming to you—workplace rights, disability, or planning documents?
- What would it feel like to know your family is protected, even in crisis?
- What one document or phone call could you take care of this week to move toward peace of mind?

Keep Pushing, Mama-You've Got This

Alright now, sweetie, we've come a long way, haven't we? You've learned a lot about your health, your strength, and how to juggle it all as a mother living with sickle cell anemia or another chronic disease. And I want you to know-each step you've taken on this journey is a step toward living your best life, no matter what this illness throws your way.

I'm not going to lie to you-there will still be tough days. Some days, you'll feel like you're fighting an uphill battle. Your body might not always cooperate, and your mind might be overwhelmed. But hear me when I say this, baby: You are stronger than you think. You've already shown that. You've survived every single challenge that's come your way so far, and you're going to keep going, one step at a time.

I know what it's like to feel like nobody really understands the struggles you're going through. I know the loneliness of trying to carry the weight of your health and your family on your shoulders. But you don't have to carry it all alone, mama. I've shared what I can with you, and I hope it's given you some tools, some comfort, and maybe even a little spark of inspiration to take charge of your life and your health.

You've got to take care of yourself because nobody else will do it for you, and your babies need you to be your healthiest, strongest self. You deserve it. And I need you to promise me something: when things get hard, and they will, you remember who you are. You remember that you are a force. You remember that you are a mother, a warrior, and a queen. And you hold your head high because there's nothing you can't handle.

You've got this, mama. You've got everything you need inside of you. So, when the pain comes, when the doubt creeps in, when life gets overwhelming, you stand tall, take a deep breath, and keep pushing forward. I believe in you. And I hope you do, too.

Now go on-love your babies, love yourself, and keep living your beautiful, resilient life. You're not just surviving-you're thriving, and that's what I want for you. So, let's make this journey one step at a time, together.

Pause & Reflect

Keep Pushing, Mama

- What have you survived that once felt impossible?
- How have you changed for the better, even in the struggle?
- What are you most proud of right now?

Write it down. Say it aloud.

And never forget—you are still becoming.

A Blessing Over You, Warrior Mama

Dear Heavenly Father,

I lift up my sister, this beautiful, brave soul reading these final words.

Thank You for her life—for every tear she's cried, every battle she's fought, and every day she's chosen to keep going. Thank You for the strength You've hidden in her, even when she couldn't feel it. Thank You for the soft places in her heart that still love, even through the pain.

Lord, I pray Your peace would surround her right now—the kind of peace that doesn't make sense but sustains.

Let her know she's never been alone. Not for a second. You've seen her in the hospital rooms, the sleepless nights, the overwhelming days, and the moments when all she could do was whisper, "Help me." And You were there. You are still here.

God, pour out Your grace in fresh measure.

Cover her home in Your protection.

Cover her body in Your healing.

Cover her children in Your promises.

Cover her heart in Your unfailing love.

Remind her that she is not defined by her diagnosis, her bank account, her to-do list, or anyone else's opinion. She is defined by You—fearfully and wonderfully made, redeemed, chosen, and called for a purpose.

I bless her mind with clarity.

I bless her spirit with joy.

I bless her body with rest.

I bless her motherhood with divine strength and softness.

I bless her future with hope, healing, and holy expectation.

And when she forgets—because we all do—gently remind her:

She is doing enough.

She is enough.

And she is still becoming all You've created her to be.

Wrap her in Your arms now, Father.

Let her rise from these pages not just informed—but empowered.

Not just encouraged—but anointed.

In the mighty and merciful name of Jesus,

Amen.

Book Club & Group Discussion Questions

1. What part of Shaundra's personal journey resonated most with you—and why?
2. How did your understanding of sickle cell anemia or chronic illness shift after reading this book?
3. Which chapter offered you the most practical tools for managing daily life?
4. In what ways did this book challenge your definition of what it means to be a "strong mom"?
5. Which section—faith, home, motherhood, healthcare, pain management, or advocacy—spoke most directly to your life?
6. What myths or misconceptions about sickle cell or chronic illness did this book help to break?
7. How do you personally define "thriving," and how does that compare with the author's definition?
8. Which self-care strategies or tips from the book would you like to try?
9. How do you think healthcare systems could better support mothers with chronic illnesses?
10. If you were to gift this book to someone, who would it be—and why?
11. What role does faith play in the author's journey, and how does it connect with your own experiences?
12. After reading this book, how might you become a better advocate—for yourself or for others?

Helpful Resources for Moms Living with SCD

Organizations offering education, community, and support:

- Sickle Cell Disease Association of America (SCDAA)

🌐 www.sicklecelldisease.org

Advocacy, education, and national support networks.

- Sickle Cell 101

🌐 www.sc101.org

Nonprofit providing medically accurate sickle cell education.

- CDC Sickle Cell Disease Resources

🌐 www.cdc.gov/ncbddd/sicklecell

Research, treatment guidelines, and patient resources.

- Hope for Sickle Cell Foundation

🌐 www.hopeforsicklecell.org

Spiritual, emotional, and social support for patients and caregivers.

- Cure Sickle Cell Initiative (NIH)

🌐 www.curesickle.org

Clinical trials and research updates for long-term solutions.

With Deepest Gratitude

First and foremost, I thank my Father in Heaven. Thank You for entrusting me with these beautiful children and revealing the vision You have for my life. Your love and guidance transcend the physical—I feel Your presence with every gentle nudge and every necessary push.

To my children—Aoki, Layla, Jayden, and Nia—thank you for giving my life its deepest meaning. You are the reason I fight, the reason I thrive, and the reason I rise every single day. I love being your momma and walking this journey with you.

To my parents—Dianne and Willard thank you for your unwavering love and support. Your resilience has been our anchor through every storm. To my family and friends—your encouragement, prayers, and presence have carried me through triumphs and trials alike.

To the hospital staff, nurses, and healthcare professionals—thank you for treating me with compassion and humanity, not just as a diagnosis. Your care made all the difference.

To the teams at St. Joseph Mercy Infusion Center, University of Michigan Hospital, Beaumont, and Beaumont Children's Hospital—thank you for bringing me home to my babies, again and again.

To the churches, community groups, and organizations who stood in the gap for my family—your generosity will never be forgotten.

And to every warrior living with a chronic illness, and every caregiver supporting someone who is—this book is for you. You are not alone.

About the Author

Shaundra M.G. Harris, known as Shaun the Mom, is a mother of four, chronic illness warrior, and fierce advocate for women balancing motherhood and health battles. Living with sickle cell anemia, she shares her story to empower other moms facing invisible struggles with visible strength.

Shaun is the founder of Shaun the Mom Publishing, a platform dedicated to helping moms rise above chronic illness, pain, and stress—one day, one page, one prayer at a time. Her writing blends experience, faith, and grit to offer hope and practical tools.

She is also the creator of The Warrior Mom Guide series, an empowering self-help collection covering topics like faith, legacy, homeschooling, budgeting, and emotional wellness.

📱 Follow Shaun the Mom: @shaunthemom (Instagram, Facebook, TikTok)

🌐 Join the Thrive Hive: A community of warrior moms supporting one another.

Coming Soon from Shaun the Mom Publishing

Children's Fiction/Fantasy
- Zarah: The Young Warrior

Memoir & Resource Guides (The Warrior Mom Guide Series)
- The Warrior Mom's Guide to Sickle Cell Anemia & Chronic Resilience
- The Warrior Mom's Guide to Generational Wealth & Family Legacy
- The Warrior Mom's Guide to Leaving a Legacy
- The Warrior Mom's Guide to Single Motherhood by Choice
- The Warrior Mom's Guide to Homeownership & Stability
- The Warrior Mom's Guide to Homeschooling for the Homegirls
- The Warrior Mom's Guide to ZBB & Cash Stuffing
- The Warrior Mom's Guide to GhettoOCD™
- The Warrior Mom's Guide to Loving Unexpectedly
- The Warrior Mom's Guide to Spiritual Reset & Chronic Faith
- The Warrior Mom's Guide to Mental Wellness & Finding Joy in the Chaos

Find books, journals, and companion resources at www.shaunthemom.com (coming soon).

Thank You for Reading :)

www.ingramcontent.com/pod-product-compliance
Lightning Source LLC
Chambersburg PA
CBHW020218170426
43201CB00007B/251